THE
PUMPKIN PLAN

THE
PUMPKIN PLAN

A Simple Strategy to Grow
a Remarkable Business in any Field

MIKE MICHALOWICZ

PORTFOLIO / PENGUIN

An imprint of Penguin Random House LLC
penguinrandomhouse.com

Most Portfolio books are available at a discount when purchased in quantity for sales promotions or corporate use. Special editions, which include personalized covers, excerpts, and corporate imprints, can be created when purchased in large quantities. For more information, please call (212) 572-2232 or e-mail specialmarkets@penguinrandomhouse.com. Your local bookstore can also assist with discounted bulk purchases using the Penguin Random House corporate Business-to-Business program. For assistance in locating a participating retailer, e-mail B2B@penguinrandomhouse.com.

LIBRARY OF CONGRESS CATALOGING IN PUBLICATION DATA
Michalowicz, Mike.
The pumpkin plan : a simple strategy to grow a remarkable business in any field / Mike Michalowicz.
p. cm.
Includes index.
ISBN 978-1-59184-488-4
1. Entrepreneurship.   2. Strategic planning.   3. Success in business.   I. Title.
HB615.M537 2012
658.4'21—dc23
2012000415

Printed in Canada
19

Book design by Sabrina Bowers

To Carly Simon. You probably think
this book is about you.
Don't you?
Don't you?

CONTENTS

CONTENTS

INTRODUCTION

Let's pretend you're in the market for a good pumpkin. You pack the kiddies in the car and drive out to the local pumpkin patch. When you get there, you see row after row after overwhelming row of orange, green and brown. You're looking for the perfect pumpkin, but they all seem to look the same. It is easy to pick out the bad ones, though—they're smashed, or dented, or bruised or look hauntingly similar to your mother-in-law.

You keep searching, and just after you get through the corn maze you spot it—the biggest pumpkin you've ever seen. It's like Charlie Brown's "Great Pumpkin" big. It's so big, it's hard to believe it's even real.

Suddenly your kids start running toward this freak of nature like it's the greatest thing ever, and you've got to admit, it kind of is. The gigantor pumpkin dwarfs all of the other pumpkins in the field. As you walk over to it, you don't even see the other pumpkins, and you wonder how you didn't spot it right off the bat. Although it is surrounded by red tape and signs saying "prize-winning pumpkin, not for sale," your kids are begging you to buy it. "Please? It's the *only* pumpkin we want!" You walk around it, marveling at its size. At its remarkableness. You get out your phone and take pictures of your kids standing next to it, and text your friends, telling them they *have* to come see the most awesome, gigantic pumpkin in the world.

Like a magnet, the pumpkin draws a continuous stream of other people, too. They pass by the other, smaller, pumpkins, their eyes glued to the orange wonder before them. The bald guy says, "How is this even possible?" The buttoned-up woman says, "It's clearly a genetic mutation." The wide-eyed grade-school boy says, "The farmer must have some super secret veggie vitamins or something." And the dazed and confused teenager says, "Dude, it looks like Jabba the Hut knocked up a basketball."

There is something absolutely irresistible, something magnetic about being the extreme. Be it the strongest, or the fastest, or the most unique. The farmer with the most extraordinary pumpkin in the field wins. Every. Single. Time.

The same is true for entrepreneurs. Yet most entrepreneurs work their tails off, only to end up with small, ordinary, unremarkable pumpkins. Compared to the giant pumpkin, the companies these struggling entrepreneurs grow are insignificant, so insignificant that customers often don't see them, or squash them, or leave them to rot in the field without a second thought.

To grow a successful business your company must be irresistibly magnetic. The average lose and are left to rot. It's the most unique—the *best*—who win.

You're probably thinking, "Duh! Do you really think I'm working my ass off to build an average company? What more do I have to do to be the best?"

Simple. You don't need to do more. You need to do different. You have to pretend you're a pumpkin farmer.

Yup. You read that right. A pumpkin farmer. But not just *any* pumpkin farmer. A freaky, geeky, overall-wearing, straw chewing pumpkin farmer, those county fair folks who dedicate their lives to growing the half-ton pumpkins you see on the evening news. Turns out that they, of all people, hold the "secret formula" for big-time entrepreneurial success: plant hearty seeds, identify the most promising pumpkins, kill off the rest of the vine, and nurture *only* the pumpkins with the biggest potential.

In this book I reveal how, by implementing the same strategies pumpkin farmers use to grow their massive gourds—and which I have, with great originality deemed "The Pumpkin Plan"—I was able to launch two multimillion-dollar companies by my thirtieth birthday, gain notoriety with top firms, and in turn help them radically grow their businesses. Not only will I share my stories and their stories of success, but, most importantly, I will teach you how to apply the same ideas and lessons to your own business.

Never forget this: Ordinary pumpkins are always forgotten. Only the giant pumpkin draws a crowd and lives on holiday cards, refrigerators and grainy YouTube videos . . . forever. The giant pumpkin is legend. And when you've grown one . . . *you* will be a legend, too.

You didn't start your business because you wanted to blend in, make enough to get by and save enough to pay for the nursing home. You went into business because you wanted to grow something amazing, something that would dramatically change the quality of your life, something that could make a difference in the world.

The late Steve Jobs has been lauded for his many accomplishments and innovations, and there's no doubt that Apple is one of the truly remarkable companies on the planet, thanks in large part to his vision. But his contribution goes beyond innovation. At the time of Jobs's death, Apple employed almost 47,000 people, hired thousands of subcontractors and, by necessity or association, inspired countless entrepreneurs to create businesses that served Apple and its customers. That is a huge contribution to our culture, one that goes way beyond how we listen to music or communicate with the world.

Now *that's* legend.

And you can grow a legendary company, too.

I know you already know this. You know that if you want to be wildly successful, you've got to be the most unique pumpkin in the patch. I didn't write this book to tell you that. I wrote this book to show you exactly *how* to grow it, to teach you a proven system that will free you from the entrepreneurial trap and create the most magnetic business in your industry.

I wrote my first book, *The Toilet Paper Entrepreneur*, for those who want to start a business but think they lack the education, resources, momentum, expertise and capital to do so. I wrote it for the millions of hopefuls who aren't afraid to work hard and take chances in order to reach their goals. And I wrote it to empower entrepreneurs with the tools they need to succeed in the start-up phase of business ownership. That book was about planting the seed; this book is about growing it . . . big-time.

Since the release of *The Toilet Paper Entrepreneur* in 2008, I've talked with thousands of entrepreneurs—at conferences I keynoted throughout the world, as an expert on various business television and radio programs, through discussions of articles I have written for publications both large and small, through my (notably whacky) blog, and face-to-face—who are looking for a way up . . . or a way out.

So I know firsthand that the sobering statistics are spot on. Entrepreneurs are struggling, trapped in a neverending cycle of sell it–do it, sell it–do it, sell it–do it that leaves them feeling desperate, hopeless, trapped. No matter how many all-nighters they pull, no matter how many kids' soccer games they miss, most entrepreneurs can't seem to get anywhere near the multimillion-dollar mark, much less beyond it.

I wrote *The Pumpkin Plan* for all of those entrepreneurs who reached out to me and said, "Help! Something's got to give." I wrote it for the entrepreneurs who are exhausted from an entrepreneurial dream that has turned into a real-life nightmare. I wrote it for the entrepreneurs who need a proven system to help them get over the hump and cruise into greatness. I wrote it for every entrepreneur who is committed to having a wildly successful business. And I wrote this book for every entrepreneur who wants to make a significant contribution to the world.

This book holds the key to your entrepreneurial liberation.

By following *The Pumpkin Plan* step by step, you will build a business that blows the competition away, magnetically attracts clients and, as clichéd as it sounds, finally gives you the life of your dreams.

CHAPTER ONE

A HALF-TON PUMPKIN IS ABOUT TO SAVE YOUR LIFE

"You don't want to be that guy, Mike."

Frank, my seventy-year-old business mentor, paused to make sure I was *really* paying attention. We'd spent all morning talking strategy and I was so overwhelmed my head felt ready to implode. Frank's a "greatest generation" Regis Philbin lookalike who wears a suit every day, even in his own house. He's so unassuming, you'd never guess he built a company worth eighty million dollars.

"What guy?" I asked.

"That old guy with only one nut left . . . hanging out of his shorts. The guy who works like a dog for fifty years and then ends up sitting in a rusty lawn chair, half-dead, with drool dripping down his chin."

Oh. *That* guy.

Frank gave it to me straight: "If you don't change your business strategy, you'll never make it. You'll kill yourself trying to build a multimillion-dollar business, but in the end you'll be a broken, bitter man living off Social Security and looking back on a lifetime of disappointment."

Wow. Okay. That would suck. So much for my retirement plan of sipping margaritas on a beach somewhere, looking at a gorgeous sunset with my gorgeous wife. Worse, I knew I was already heading in that direction. Five years as an entrepreneur under my belt and I had nothing. Well, almost nothing—I still had both of my nuts . . . so far.

I was a freakin' slave to my business and all I had to show for it was stress-induced red blotches all over my face (never did find out what those were). The hours were insane, and when I did spend time with my wife and our five-year-old son, it was fake time—I was on my laptop, or on the phone, or talking business, or thinking about business—completely unfocused on the two most important people in my life. I was completely out of balance. Maybe you're familiar with this scenario. Maybe you're *intimately* familiar with it. Maybe you've got red blotch grossness on your face, too.

In four years Olmec, my computer technology company, had grown from nonexistent to almost one million dollars in revenue. Huge, right? Nope. Total bullshit. Our costs were so high, our cash so *not* flowing, that bringing in close to a million felt like a joke—a cruel, cruel joke. Gross revenue means nothing when your receptionist makes more than you do. I could barely support my family and I was under constant pressure to make payroll so that everyone on my team could support *their* families.

I suffered from the "if only" disease that plagues most midstage entrepreneurs. I kept thinking, "If only I could work harder" or "If only I had an investor" or "If only I could land one big client, I'd be living the dream." So I pushed on, and on, and on, believing I was *this close* to making it. But like a hamster on a wheel, I was working my ass off and getting nowhere. *Something had to give.* I didn't want to end up a one-nut drool factory.

I sighed, pulled out my notebook and said, "Okay, Frank. What do I have to do?"

WHAT GOT YOU HERE
WON'T GET YOU THERE

The idea for Olmec started where most brilliant ideas are born— in a bar. (Raise your hand if you wrote your first business plan on a beer-stained cocktail napkin. I thought so.) I was twenty-three at the time, and I worked as a technician at a computer services com- pany. One Friday night I went out to blow off steam with Chris, my friend since kindergarten. I was pissed at my boss—for what, I don't remember—but really, I was looking for a way out. My rant quickly progressed from, "I'm smarter than him, I work harder than him, and I know more about this business than he does" to "The boss is an asshole!" Fourteen (cheap) drinks later, Chris and I had agreed to quit our damn jobs and start our own damn com- puter services business . . . damn it.

It was a classic retaliation story, and I very quickly figured out that this scenario has (at least) three problems. First, while liquid courage can help you get over your initial fears, planning a busi- ness in a drunken stupor completely obliterates all rational thought, which, as it turns out, you need to start a business. (Go figure.) Second, there's a lot more to running a business than just showing up and doing the work. (Who knew?) Third, and perhaps most annoying of all, owning your own business will not automatically free you from the grind that inspired you to get drunk in the first place. (Surprise!)

Remember when you started your business, all amped up on adrenalin and hope? Your dream was huge, *epic*, because you need a big-ass dream to pull you off the wannabe couch and actually do something awesome. When I closed my eyes, I could see my dream in full color: I was a millionaire, at the helm of a mega-successful company, living the good life without a care in the world.

But when I opened my eyes, the harsh reality set in. We had no clients, and worse, we had no idea how to get them. So you can imagine why, within a week of quitting my job, I was consumed by fear. Total. Complete. Soul-quaking fear. You know the constant "I'm a failure" thoughts that run around in your head while you struggle to do something great? Well, they ran through my head like a weather warning at the bottom of the TV screen. What if I can't sell? What if I fail? What if I have to crawl back to my asshole boss and beg for my job back?

Fear propelled me to take action. There was no other option. Except for one little problem: I had no idea how to get clients. So I started knocking on doors. Literally. (What? That's how they do it in the movies, right? *Old* movies.) I went after any and all clients—big, small, near, far, taxidermists to insurance agents— and said yes to any of them who expressed the least bit of interest in what I had to offer, no matter what their demands.

"Will I drive six hours to install your computer mouse? No problem."

"Would I give you a fifty-percent discount and a 120-day net? Absolutely."

"Could I service your ancient computer system, even though I know nothing about it and will have to spend two days reading the twelve-inch-thick manual . . . that's written in French . . . by a Chinese guy who doesn't speak French? Sure. Why not?"

In those first few months after we launched, both Chris and I ran around like Tasmanian devils. Did I keep regular hours? Sure I did. If I was awake, I worked. Regularly. I had no pride, so to save money I pulled all-nighters, or slept in clients' offices. I moved my wife and five-year-old son into the only safe place I could afford— an apartment in a retirement building, where the average age was somewhere between eighty and dead (most, I believe, were slightly older than dead) and where the residents got up at three in the morning to vacuum, or pace the floor, or watch PBS so loud only deaf people could stand it. And, if you haven't put one and one together, most of them *were* deaf.

Olmec started making decent money, then better money, then good money. But no matter how much money the company made, we still had very little left over. And even though we now *had* clients, I still worked five to nine (that's a.m. to p.m.) eight days a week. I still chased after clients. I still said yes to every Tom, Dick and Harriet who called. The punishing grind *never let up*.

After two years in business, I hit the wall. I was a burned-out, unhealthy mess, and so was Chris. But still, the fear of failing and losing everything kept me going. This was right about the time the sexy red splotches showed up on my face. In our family Christmas photos, my face had more color on it than the tree. Still, like a lunatic, I kept telling myself, "There *has* to be a sweet spot, a moment when this business shifts into second gear and all of this hard work pays off." To me, the solution was clear: Just keep racing the engine; work harder and harder till it breaks or I break.

Two years later, in 2000, the Small Business Administration (SBA) named me New Jersey's Young Entrepreneur of the Year. A heartbeat later, the president of a prestigious bank offered me a $250,000 expansion loan. So I must have been raking it in, right? Nope. To the outside world it looked like I *was* living the dream, but the truth was, nothing much had changed. I was still chained to my business, pushing just as hard as I always had. No matter how much we earned, money was still tight. I thought, "If being an entrepreneur leads to wealth, why am I so freakin' broke?"

Enter Frank, my personal Yoda. I met him at my first ever chamber of commerce meeting. In a room full of overconfident, desperate salesmen, he was the only guy who didn't pitch me. He just sat in a corner and watched. He really didn't care if you hired him to coach you. He didn't have to care—as president of a major medical services company, he had taken the company from $8 million to $80 million without breaking a sweat, so he didn't need the work, or the money. This was his fun stage of life—he wanted to coach (maybe adopt is a better word) young entrepreneurs.

I did hire him, and I tried to follow his advice. (Really, I did.) I tried to become Frank's definition of an entrepreneur, which, I later learned, is the *only* definition of an entrepreneur: "You're not an entrepreneur yet, Mike. Entrepreneurs don't do most of the work. Entrepreneurs identify the problems, discover the opportunities and then build processes to allow *other people and other things* to do the work." But since my main objective was getting more clients and keeping them happy, I was a C student at best.

Frank is the type of guy who loves white boards and charts and graphs. Maybe I was getting high off the dry-erase markers, but every time he coached me, I left feeling dazed and confused. What Frank said made sense, but I could not see how to *do* what he told me. He mapped out Point B, and I was at Point A, and I couldn't see the line that connected the two. Later, I would make a half-assed effort to apply his strategies . . . when I had time, which I never did.

It was in one of his coaching sessions that he showed me a glimpse of my wretched colostomy bag of a future. Frank said, "If you don't want to end up like the one-nut guy, you're going to have to cut your client list."

Cut our client list? Was he crazy? I busted my ass for that client list. If anything, we needed *more* clients. How would we make it if I started cutting clients?

"List your clients in order of revenue," Frank told me. "Then, take your top-paying clients and separate them into two categories: great clients and everyone else, from the ho-hum clients to the clients who annoy you so much, you cringe when they call you. Keep the great, top-paying clients, and cut the rest. Every single one."

Yowza! Frank was crazy. He must've been the one sniffin' the dry-erase markers. I told myself that if I get rid of all the clients who make me cringe or who don't bring in the big bucks, I won't make enough money. I'll have to fire people; I'll have to close the big office and get a small one . . . or, more likely, I'll have to get a third-shift job at Denny's.

I could see it was a simple strategy. And it had obviously worked for Frank. Frank had the proof: boatloads of cash. Legit. Liquid. Assets. But still, it scared the crap out of me. I just couldn't wrap my head around actually getting rid of the clients I had worked so hard to find and keep happy. It seemed absolutely crazy—saying no to a client, to money, to potential referrals . . .

But ending up like the one-nut guy scared me *more*.

I did follow Frank's advice—sort of. I drafted a rough list of great clients and not-so-great clients. I happily fired a few jerkwad clients who'd taken advantage of me about a thousand times too many. But I didn't fully commit. The thing is, Frank had given me a lot of homework, and finishing all of it while chasing after clients—yes, I still wanted more clients—proved to be impossible.

Every time I tried to focus on "the list" I got distracted putting out fires, or dealing with demanding customers, or juggling payments so I could cover payroll. Like most entrepreneurs, I was the jack-of-all-trades. I wore the term "workaholic" like a badge of courage. And because I never made it out of survival mode, I still ran the business—and my life—with the same frenzied energy. The one-nut guy haunted my dreams. He sat on my shoulder and taunted me with his relentless cackle. Yeah, that's right, he sat on my shoulder . . . and I don't even want to tell you where his nut was hanging.

Okay, I was mental, but not *that* mental. I knew the one-nut guy was a figment of my stress-induced delirium. But I did worry. Would I *ever* get off the grind? Would I ever make the kind of dough people *thought* I made? Or would I end up toothless, drooling, bald, blotchy and broke?

Then one day, a half-ton pumpkin saved my life.

THE HOLY GRAIL IN THE PUMPKIN PATCH

It was October, and the local newspaper ran an article about a farmer who grew a gigantic, prize-winning pumpkin. This guy was not your typical farmer. He was a geek farmer, obsessed with growing mongo pumpkins. He'd dedicated his life to breaking the state record, and there he was, perched on his flatbed truck, smiling like he'd won the lottery, with the biggest-ass pumpkin I've ever seen right behind him. I just had to know—how the hell did he get the pumpkin to grow to mammoth, half-ton, blue-ribbon size?

Here's how the article broke down the pumpkin-growing process:

STEP ONE: Plant promising seeds.

STEP TWO: Water, water, water.

STEP THREE: As they grow, routinely remove all of the diseased or damaged pumpkins.

STEP FOUR: Weed like a mad dog. Not a single green leaf or root permitted if it isn't a pumpkin plant.

STEP FIVE: When they grow larger, identify the stronger, faster-growing pumpkins. Then, remove all the less-promising pumpkins. Repeat until you have one pumpkin on each vine.

STEP SIX: Focus all of your attention on the big pumpkin. Nurture it around the clock like a baby, and guard it like you would your first Mustang convertible.

STEP SEVEN: Watch it grow. In the last days of the season, this will happen so fast you can actually *see* it happen.

Holy crap, I thought. Pumpkin farmers hold the secret formula for big-time entrepreneurial success. My get-out-of-jail-free card. The Holy Grail. The missing link. My golden ticket. (Yes, it was all of those things to me, and more, so much more.) There it was, in black and white . . . and orange. The answer I'd been looking for, for years. I needed to treat my company like a giant pumpkin!

In case you're wondering if I'd officially lost it, here's what I understood when I read the article:

STEP ONE: Identify and leverage your biggest natural strengths.

STEP TWO: Sell, sell, sell.

STEP THREE: As your business grows, fire all of your small-time, rotten clients.

STEP FOUR: Never, ever let distractions—often labeled as new opportunities—take hold. Weed 'em out fast.

STEP FIVE: Identify your top clients and remove the rest of your less-promising clients.

STEP SIX: Focus all your attention on your top clients. Nurture and protect them; find out what they want more than anything, and if it's in alignment with what you do best, give it to them. Then, replicate that same service or product for as many of the same types of top client as possible.

STEP SEVEN: Watch your company grow to a giant size.

With the visual of this pumpkin farmer watering, feeding, loving, guarding and caring for his one big pumpkin to the exclusion of everything else, my next steps became crystal clear. His maniacal focus on growing huge pumpkins was second only to that of a serial killer, and all he did was follow this simple formula over and over again and he grew crazy big pumpkins. If I followed the same method the farmer used to grow giant pumpkins, a method rooted (pardon the pun) in Frank's "client list" strategy, and focused on my top clients like a crazed farmer, I could grow my business to be a giant "pumpkin," too. It was clear now. This was the path from today (Point A) to where I wanted to be (Point B).

I finally had my first major "duh" moment. The fear-driven strategy that got Olmec just shy of a million in gross revenue wasn't going to get us to *millions* in gross revenue. Frank's advice started to make sense. The say-yes-to-everyone strategy could not be sustained over time, and it was actually stunting growth. I was spread too thin, wasting energy serving clients who made me crazy and would never make me rich; and in serving them I was taking precious time away from the clients with whom I enjoyed working, and who *could* make me rich.

I was also using my time to handle things that didn't come naturally to me, when I should have been focused on doing the few things I did well. I was writing advertising and marketing messages to get everyone and their mother to walk through our door. I was doing new work for rotten clients, trying to figure out how to serve them better. I was ignoring my best clients, who were just starting to grow. Instead of watering them, I was throwing seeds on top of them, crowding them out. Always seeding, hardly watering. Never weeding, and never nurturing.

I knew I was really good at figuring out how to serve clients better and at developing systems to replicate that service—but how could I do that for my best clients if I was so busy trying to keep my rotten clients—all of whom wanted different things—happy?

Once you've moved past the early stages of entrepreneurship, success isn't a quantity game anymore. If I wanted my business to dwarf the competition, I would have to cut the clients who were actually holding me back, cut the aspects of my business that weren't serving growth and find unparalleled ways to serve my best clients. Like a geeky, freaky farmer of mammoth pumpkins, I would focus all of my attention, time, love, support, creativity and energy on the most promising clients in my "patch."

I shared my revelation with Chris and we followed the Pumpkin Plan in earnest. Almost immediately, everything became easier. We saw results lightning fast—so fast that within a couple of months, I was able to jump off the hamster wheel for good and stop freaking out. Our top clients felt like rock stars. Our employees were happy. Our bottom line moved up a few notches. Then a few more. And then, for the first time in four years, I felt like a real entrepreneur. You know, the kind of person who takes a risk and makes it happen.

We weren't millionaires yet, but now I knew there was a better way to become one. And man, I was on fire! I tweaked the Pumpkin Plan, made it my own, and in that process I truly fell in love with the art of entrepreneurship. Scratch that—I fell in love with the *science* of entrepreneurship.

Two years after I implemented my first Pumpkin Plan I opted to let Chris buy me out so I could go my own way. I wanted to apply the Pumpkin Plan from the ground up. The very next day I started a new, different company. Chris continued to apply the Pumpkin Plan and Olmec is doing so well they're practically printing money, and in a crappy economy, no less.

And me? Well, folks, I became one of those oddballs . . . those freaky pumpkin-farmer types who obsesses and obsesses over one thing—growing super successful businesses. I tweaked my revised Pumpkin Plan over time, improving systems, and within two years, eleven months and eight days (but who's counting?) I sold my second company for millions to a Fortune 500 firm.

Kiss my ass, one-nut guy.

Work the Plan—
Take Action in 30 Minutes (or Less)

I. *Find the "why."* If your dream is to just be big and get rich, that's not enough to grow a significant, successful business. Ask yourself why you started this business and not another business. What purpose are you serving? What gets you stoked? If you know your "why," it will resonate with your clients. More importantly, it will be your compass, and boy oh boy, do you need one of those. (Have you ever tried to find your way out of a forest without one?)

2. *Set a revenue "pulse" goal for this year.* In order to get the heart of your business beating again (meaning you can survive without perpetual panic), how much revenue do you need to generate? Don't put yourself last on the list. Start by figuring out what you personally need to be comfortable, to know that you're back on your feet. Then figure out how much revenue your company needs to make to actually support that.

3. *Ask better questions.* Really big pumpkins have really strong roots. We can only find the best answers when we ask great questions. Rather than ask, "Why do I struggle?" ask, "How can I take home $2,000 a day, every day?" Either way, your brain will find the answer. Write down the one big, bad question you always ask when you're beating your head against the wall, and then reverse it.

4. *Get the supporting Pumpkin Plan materials.* There are more resources, including new discoveries I've had, available for download right now. Go to PumpkinPlanYourBiz.com to get it. It will be 30 seconds well-spent.

About the stories in this book

I love a good story. So I wrote a bunch of them to help you envision how you could Pumpkin Plan any industry, even—no, *especially*—

yours. These stories use all of the strategies detailed in this book, including stuff you haven't read yet, and are denoted with the title "How To Pumpkin Plan Your Industry."

And to be clear, I made them up so you can see the endless possibilities the Pumpkin Plan offers. The stories follow each chapter and are designed to show you that the Pumpkin Plan formula works, no matter how tough your competition is, no matter how much (or how little) money you have in the bank, no matter how many clients you have (or don't have). It just works.

Each story includes examples about how to employ most or all of the strategies detailed in this book, not just those explored in that chapter. So you may want to go back and re-read the stories after you've finished the book and learned all about how to Pumpkin Plan your business.

And just so we're *absolutely clear*, there are loads of true stories in this book, too—both about me and about other people. They are woven into each chapter as real-world examples of entrepreneurs who rocked some aspect of the Pumpkin Plan to great effect. For the true stories, I name names. Obviously, none of these scenarios will match yours 100 percent, but I hope you find them inspiring, or at least, thought-provoking.

Enjoy!

How to Pumpkin Plan Your Industry — Travel

Let's pretend you're a partner in a small airline. Stow your carry-on, fasten your seat belt and put your tray into an upright position, we're going to Pumpkin Plan your industry!

Your airline can't compete with the big boys or girls, or even with the medium-sized airlines. You've got fifteen planes running short routes to and from major cities like New York, Boston, Philadelphia and Washington, D.C. Your planes are never full, unless there's a problem with another airline. Hardly anyone even knows the name of your company—Big East Airlines.

You try to compete on price, but Southwest and JetBlue have you beat. You try to compete on convenience, but United, Delta and American have more planes, more flight options and more everything else, so they have you beat. You try to compete on rocking it out with cool extras and stuff, but Virgin America has you beat on that by a mile. You try to compete on all three at the same time, and that's when things get hairy. Like, *really* hairy, as in Chapter 11-on-the-horizon hairy. You're killing yourself trying to get an edge over the competition by playing their game, following their curve. You can blame it on the economy or the price of gas all you want, but Big East Airlines is going down.

That is, until you decide to Pumpkin Plan your business. You start with the Assessment Chart, which you have trouble filling out because you really don't have a lot of repeat business. Still, you follow through and realize that your worst customers are tourists who make unreasonable demands in-flight—better movies, new headsets, more snacks—and only use you when you have a half-off promotion or some other limited-time offer. You really, *really* don't want to fire any clients, because you're clamoring for passengers. But you want to save your business, and then grow the heck out of it, so you do it anyway. It's pretty easy to get rid of this type of client; once the special discounts are gone, so are the "diseased" clients.

You figure out that your best customers are last-minute customers, the passengers who, ironically, only use you because they have a last-minute meeting and every other airline is booked. There's no built-in loyalty with these customers—most of them will never fly with you again. Still, you call ten of them up with the goal of getting their Wish List.

When you ask, "What could we do better?" they say, "Nothing." When you ask, "What frustrates you about my industry?" they say, "Nothing." Hmm. This is going to be a little tougher than you thought it would be. Thinking on your feet, you say, "What frustrates you most about traveling?"

And that's when the dam bursts. Suddenly you're getting an earful of complaints about how, because of transportation to the airport and the security line, it takes half a day to take a one-hour flight. Your top clients, the last-minute travelers who use you only when there is no other option, are all business executives and professionals living in the suburbs of major cities, and they lose productivity when they travel. They can't work in the back of a cab. They can't work when they're driving to the airport. They can't work when they're standing in the insanely long TSA line.

You thank them for their input, and then start brainstorming with your team. How could you turn their frustrations into a 180-degree turn for Big East Airlines? You ask a bunch of really awesome questions, but the one that sticks is, "What if we could cut the time it takes to get *to the flight* in half, or better?" You come up with a great solution to run buses out to pick up passengers at various locations, buses that can use the *carpool* fast lane. And unlike the other airport bus companies, you'll take them directly to the Big East Airlines entrance. And because they lose precious time traveling to the airport, you'll outfit each bus with tray tables, outlets and WiFi for laptops.

You decide to run the idea by a few of the clients who shared their frustrations with you, and they love the idea, but not enough to break up with their favorite airline and start going steady with yours. So you go back to the drawing board, and add a few other key points. First, you work out a deal with the local churches in your pick-up areas, allowing the commuters to park their cars in their empty lots for free, Monday through Friday. (You pay the churches a fee, of course.) Then, you assign a gate agent to every bus, and check everyone in when they get on the bus. If they have luggage to check, you just do it right there, stow it in the bus and have skycaps take it to the baggage scan *for them* when they arrive at the airport.

Then, you decide to pull out all the stops and create a dedicated security line just for your passengers. You have to pay a premium for this, but it will be worth it if you can make your top clients' dreams come true.

With your revised plan in place, you go back to these clients again and ask for more advice. When you hear, "When will you start implementing this new system?" you know you're on to something.

Knowing that your top clients would rather be super productive than be entertained on their flights, you get rid of the in-flight movie and radio your eliminated clients wanted, but were never quite happy with. Then, you get rid of the kiddie snacks. Now you've eliminated expenses related to unwanted clients, and you can funnel some of that into offering *free* WiFi on the plane, or concierge service, or a live feed of CNN or MSNBC.

Before you roll out your new fancy service, you decide it's time to stand out from the crowd, time to stop competing with all of the other airlines. So you re-label yourself. Now you're Elite Commuter Express—you're not even calling yourself an airline anymore. Your niche is business folks who don't want to waste their time getting to and from the airport, and you've got a *lock* on that service. You invented it!

Your top clients, who probably took your first call because they were stuck in a cab and had nothing better to do, now want to sign up for your VIP club and start booking flights immediately. They identify with your new name, because *they are commuters*. They start telling everyone about your service, and now most of your flights are full well in advance.

You start moving in concentric circles, placing ads in entrepreneurial magazines, in *The Wall Street Journal* and on popular business-focused blogs. You sponsor charity golf and tennis tournaments in the suburban communities where your top clients live. You show up at trade shows geared toward entrepreneurs.

Then, you launch an Under-Promise, Over-Deliver (UPOD) program that knocks the blazers right off of your (now happy as clams) top clients. You make deals with other companies who cater to executives and commuters, and offer product testing on your planes. You're passing out noise-canceling headphones, top-quality pens, new wireless cards, cell phones—it's like Christmas on the freakin' *Oprah Winfrey Show* on your plane. But not all the time. Passengers never know when they will be given a new product . . . which means your flights are *always* full.

Before you know it, Elite Commuter Express is *the* go-to airline for business executives and entrepreneurs on the East Coast. Your service is so unforgettable, you get frequent press about it, and soon you're getting requests to expand your service for routes to and from Los Angeles, Las Vegas and San Francisco. (Good thing you changed your name to Commuter Express . . . Big East Airlines running routes on the *West* Coast just doesn't fly, does it?)

And how about your prices? You are dictating top dollar now. Cutting travel time in half—and cutting aggravation completely—is worth a lot of green.

Guess what? You're going to need more planes.

CHAPTER TWO

A SLOW, MISERABLE DEATH

I met Bruce while I was coaching my son's soccer team. I guess he recognized me because he made a beeline for me after the game. Bruce is an aging, *Jersey Shore* type who looks like he was probably pretty ripped back in the day. "I read *The Toilet Paper Entrepreneur* and I've been following you for three years," he said. (I can't tell you how thrilled I am to meet readers of *TPE*, and how grateful I am to hear how the book may have helped them. It is exciting and humbling all at the same time, because it is the fulfillment of what I have defined as my life's purpose. And when people ask me to autograph their book . . . I practically soil myself—it is the "rock star" moment that I dreamed of since childhood. Not the soiling part. The autograph part.)

After I thanked Bruce, he said, "I need you. I didn't know how to approach you, but this seems like serendipity, so . . ."

Bruce explained that although he was bringing in $700,000 a year in revenue, he was nearly bankrupt. A florist for weddings and other events, he also rented out equipment for weddings and operated a showroom/retail space that leased space to other wedding vendors. I agreed to meet him at the showroom later that week.

As he gave me a tour of the space, Bruce told me he's so broke, he's had to borrow money from his parents. (To be clear, he's no college kid who bit off more than he could chew. He's been at this for twenty years.) I ask, "Of the vendors you lease space to, who is making the most money?" Turns out, the photographer is making the most, by a mile. He's got the tiniest little space in the showroom, yet he's bringing in ten times as much as Bruce does. And, believe it or not, Bruce typically deals with the photographer's clients for him . . . because he's too busy working to *show up* at the showroom.

Bruce wears so many hats, he's not only broke, he's a freakin' mess-o-stress. No big shocker here—there is always a direct correlation between diluted focus and a diluted bank account.

As we settle into his expensive showroom furniture for a brief "next steps" chat, he's saying all the right things: "Things have to change. I can't go on this way. I have to focus." But I know he's not ready. He *thinks* he's ready because his life is a train wreck, but really he's just desperate. He feels defeated, but not enough to make the hard, bold decisions that will help him save his business. How do I know he's not ready? Because out of the corner of my eye I can see his Cadillac Escalade parked outside. If I were in his position, that sucker would have been sold ages ago.

When our businesses are in a state of collapse, entrepreneurs go through three stages. First, we deny that we're struggling. You know what I am talking about. Someone asks how your business is going and you say, "Great! Just landed a big client!" But inside you can feel your lungs compress as the stress builds. Things aren't great. Money is draining away, fast. But you're afraid to admit you're struggling because what if people think you're not capable? What if future prospects ignore you? What if your team begins to doubt you? In Stage One of the collapse, entrepreneurs deny the truth because our egos can't handle it.

Only when the business is knocking on death's door do we admit that we're struggling. Enter Stage Two. For many, the stress at this point has become a fact of life. Wake up stressed. Go to bed stressed. Have stressful dreams. Stress about being stressed. Repeat over and over. In some perverted way, you start to be proud of how stressed you are. "You think you have it bad?" you say. "Well, let me just tell you how crappy my life is." Even at this stage, no corrective action happens because people get temporary relief by blowing off steam and reciting their sob stories. It looks a little different, but it's still ego.

In Stage Three we just throw our hands in the air (there's that defeatism again) and say, "Life sucks," as if fate had anything to do it (it doesn't) and our success or failure is completely out of our hands (it isn't). You know this stage—it's the one where you shake your fist at the sky and shout, "Why me? Why am I being punished? Why can't I catch a break?" (with maybe a few colorful expletives thrown in). This is the point at which most people give in. They stop making an effort but continue working—strike that, *slaving*—and accept that it will never get better. All the fight is gone.

Bruce was a classic example of someone in the "life sucks" stage, but his behavior hadn't changed to reflect his situation— hence the pimped-out ride. Many entrepreneurs continue on like this, year after year, always behind the eight ball, under constant stress, doing the same shit they've been doing since day one.

Nothing changes; nothing is on an upward trajectory except their blood pressure . . . and debt . . . and taxes. But that's *it*.

A few weeks after our first meeting, I agreed to meet Bruce for a beer and talk about his options. He said, "I can't afford to pay you, but I need you." I could see from his haggard appearance that the imminent demise of his business had taken a toll on his health. As a practice I rarely do any business coaching, and I have never done it for free. I don't know why, but I agreed to take on Bruce's case.

"I've never done this before, and I will never do this again, but I will help you for the cost of this one beer," I said. (There has to be an exchange of some sort, even if it's only a glass of tap.) A look of relief washed over Bruce's face. I went on, "I will work with you for three sessions. I will be absolutely clear with you about what you need to do to save your business, beginning with killing all of these bullshit costs—including the car. All the unnecessary expenses—gone. All of the side projects—gone. All of the clients who are really the *other vendor's* clients—gone."

As I laid out exactly how we would Pumpkin Plan his business, Bruce's expression changed. He looked concerned. Maybe even a little scared. I could see his mind rolling over the expenses he "had" to keep, the projects he "had" to keep alive, the chaos he "had" to keep feeding. "You will resist me," I said. "But if you follow my plan, you will save your company." I wanted to add, "and your life," but since he seemed overwhelmed enough already, I decided against it.

And then he said the words I hear every day from entrepreneurs all over the world: "But I'm just one client away from making it. I've just got to close that one big deal."

Nope. Bruce wasn't ready. He still thought all he needed was one killer client and all of his problems would be solved. Problem was, he'd been one client away from making it *for twenty years.*

No matter how much Bruce wanted these words to be true, *believed* these words *were* true, they weren't. And they never are. No one is ever one deal away from making it. You might be one payment away from saving your ass—this week—but making it? No. To really make it, to become the industry leader you set out to become, you need a sound business to begin with. You need strong roots, a carefully planned, efficient infrastructure, a maniacal focus on the one thing you do very, very well. Rather than fix what's not working, you need to cut it out like the cancer it is. Then, you need to expand on what *is* working.

People like Bruce aren't really trying to "make it" make it; they're just trying to make it to next Tuesday.

Eric, on the other hand, is making it just fine—at first glance. A Formula1 race car driver, engineer and all-around racing maven, Eric started driving very young (barely legal) and doggedly pursued a career in the industry. Over the past twenty years he has built up quite a business. You know those twenty-four-hour races? He wins them. You know those big exhibitions put on by luxury car manufacturers like Porsche? He helps launch them. You know those driving schools where everyday schmucks (ahem . . . me) can come and learn how to drive Formula1 cars? He develops them. As a race engineer, he also helps drivers win races. And he makes deals. Lots of 'em.

The only problem is, Eric's business is pretty much just Eric. While he does build and manage teams who handle much of the grunt work for him, he's still pretty much a one-man band. You see, early on in Eric's career, he had an epiphany. "I realized the chances of becoming a superstar driver were about the same as becoming a movie star, and I noticed that the people who stayed in one specialized area of racing rarely made the kind of money I needed to make to support my family," he told me. "So I learned how to do all of it really, really well."

As we talked, I couldn't help but notice Eric's constant refrain: "I do everything I do to support my family." Now, I realize that I'm an amateur observer of human behavior at best, but I have seen this before. Refrains are defense. Something in his heart is out of sync with his actions, and his mind is trying to protect him. Eric wasn't repeating this because I needed to believe it; he was repeating it because *he* needed to believe it. The realization that his real sacrifice was his freedom and time with his family would be too much to handle.

Eric is all work, all the time. And he is the go-to guy for, well, just about everything to do with Formula1 racing. Calling me from a track in Wisconsin just two days before he heads out to a track in Montreal, Eric explains why people hire him. "I can tell you exactly how much everything costs—the trailer, the tires, the tent we're standing under, the payroll for every one of these guys, everything—and I can tell you the details of the sponsorship deal, and if the driver is ready, and how the car tests, and what needs to be tweaked and which engineer is the best person to tweak it. I'm not here because I know one thing inside and out; I'm here because I know everything inside and out."

When I ask Eric to tell me one thing that helped him become financially successful, he says, "Early on I decided on a rule for myself: always answer the damn phone. I used to rack up $3,000 cell phone bills keeping up with this. If it rings in the middle of the night, I answer it. If it rings in the middle of dinner, I answer it. My clients know they can *always* get me, and that has helped my business tremendously."

I can see that. I get that. But I also know that this commitment has put Eric's clients center stage in his life. He's running himself ragged trying to keep up with all of the financial success, all of the new opportunities, all of the potential.

Eric is making more money than most people in his field, and he has sustained a career in a highly-competitive industry he absolutely loves. This wouldn't be a problem if Eric wasn't perpetually working, missing out on time with his family, answering phone calls from clients 24-7. He's become a slave to his business because it is a hundred percent dependent on him—his knowledge, his contacts, his unique approach to racing. Eric has fallen into the other trap—trading time for money. He's maxed out. He has no balance, becoming more machine than man. The irony.

He's just as stuck as Bruce is, only he makes more money.

When I asked Eric how he could scale his business he said, "When you figure it out, let me know." Like so many one-man bands, Eric believes his knowledge and skill set isn't teachable, and if you can't teach it, you can't systematize it. And if you can't systematize it, you can't grow it. Period. If you're making good money doing what you do, you can get stuck in the mindset that you're the only person on the planet who can do what you do. You become blind to the trap you set for yourself.

I share Eric's story to show you that there is a second way to be stuck. Like Eric, you may be doing just fine. You might earn more than enough to live a good life. You may not have debt or cash flow challenges. You might be in high demand within your industry; you might love what you do. But if your business is dependent on *you* doing all the work, or even most of it, you'll never grow a giant pumpkin. Remember Frank's definition of an entrepreneur: *Entrepreneurs identify the problems, discover the opportunities and then build processes to allow other people and other things to get it done.*

Like you, Bruce and Eric had dreams when they first started out. I'm not sure what Bruce's dream looked like exactly, but his Escalade is a big clue. He probably wanted to "make it big" and "live the life," complete with all of the trappings of success. And Eric—well, I do know what he wanted, because he told me: "I got started because I just loved racing." Eric is in it for the pure joy of it, for the thrill of it, because he's a competitor, because he is made to win.

Whether you're barely getting by, doing "okay" or seriously looking for a way out (like now, please), you're probably thinking that once-promising entrepreneurial dream is just a fantasy, something for the lucky few (or the silver-spooned—yeah, I am talking to you, Donald Trump). Even if it were possible for you to dominate your industry and rake in buckets of cash, you'd probably die trying. Who has the time? You certainly don't. You're already working twenty-five hours a day, eight days a week. You rarely see your family, and when you do make time for your daughter's dance recital or happy hour with your buds, you're not there. Not really. You're thinking about the latest problem and how you're going to fix it.

Every second of your waking life is spent trying to figure out how to hang on to this fledgling business of yours. You're busy wearing all of your many hats, worrying about making payroll and if Social Security will be enough to keep you in ramen noodles when you retire. Who the hell has time to go for the dream when you barely have the time or the money to eat?

Can you even remember the dream?

Let me refresh your memory.

You want the freedom to live, work and express yourself as you choose. You want the power to influence the marketplace, your culture, your community. You want to make a difference. You want to grow something amazing from nothing, something people want and love and rave about. You want to succeed in the truest sense of the word.

And if all of that translates to you earning heaps and heaps of cash, all the better.

Instead, you're a slave to your business. It owns you—and it's kicking your ass. And if you're being really honest, even though the rest of the world thinks you're a big-time (or rising) entrepreneur, sometimes it feels like your business is quicksand and you're sinking down right in the middle of it, not a tree branch in sight.

Every day, I see a media story or read a blog post about how entrepreneurs are poised to jump-start the world economy. In reality, many entrepreneurs are poised to jump off a bridge. In case you've missed the news for the last few years—which, considering your schedule, is a good possibility—each year, according to the U.S. Department of Labor, Americans start one million new businesses, and yet nearly eighty percent of these businesses fail within the first five years. Eighty percent, people.

The problem is, entrepreneurs are stuck. Bruce is stuck because he's a slave to money (because he doesn't have it) and Eric is stuck because he's a slave to time (because he doesn't have enough of it). You're stuck because . . . well, you tell me.

Not sure if you're stuck? Let's find out.

If you've heard yourself say, "If I could just get one more client (or project or deal or major sale), I would finally make it," or if your business is dependent on you to *do the work,* or if you think your dream is just that—a dream—you're trapped. But I know a way out. A way out for Bruce. For Eric. For you.

You're not going to want to do some of the things I call on you to do in this book. Like Bruce, you'll resist part or all of my advice. Like Eric, you will tell me it can't be done in your industry "because it is so unique"—or specialized, or different. You'll hold out on me (and yourself) and pick and choose which steps you'll skip over, and which steps you'll follow. Not because it seems too good to be true, but because so much of what I have to say—what I *know* to be true—goes against your natural instincts. This stuff may mess with your ego a bit, challenge your self-perception and maybe even freak you out.

So if you're not sure if you should continue, ask yourself one question:

Do you want your business to die a slow, miserable death?

I'm just going to go ahead and assume you've answered no. I'm not trying to be harsh, but it's important for you to understand that unless you're already the best, unless you're dominating your industry, unless you aren't suffocating under a weight of bills and expectations, there's a good chance you'll end up the one-nut guy. And I really, *really* don't want to see that happen to you. I hate that guy.

Work the Plan—
Take Action in 30 Minutes (or Less)

I. *Revisit the dream.* You had a dream once, and you knew exactly what your life would look like, exactly what you would do with your buckets of cash, and exactly how you would feel when you pulled it off. When all you can think about is how to cover next week's payroll, that dream may seem out of reach. Still, it's that dream that keeps you from giving up. You need that dream now, more than ever. So, right now, revisit the dream that inspired you to launch your company in the first place. Write it down and keep it handy to review it . . . because we're about to make it happen.

2. *Commit to me!* Now that you are clear on your dream, you need to make it public, baby! I want to hear about it and hold you accountable, Pumpkin Plan style. Email me at Mike@MikeMichal owicz.com with the subject line "My Pumpkin Plan Dream," so I can easily find it. In your email, include some of the details from what you wrote down in step one. I read and reply to every one of my emails (seriously), but sometimes it takes me a little while to respond, so just be patient.

How to Pumpkin Plan Your Industry — Online

Let's pretend you're an online retailer, selling costume jewelry. Tear your eyes away from your stats, push those packing boxes to one side and let's Pumpkin Plan your business!

You've got a nice little business selling original and reproduction costume jewelry online. You have the flexibility of working from home, which means you get to spend more time with your kids, and you love that. But you're not making nearly as much money as you'd like to make, as you *thought* you'd make, and every time you stay up until three in the morning stuffing boxes you begin to wonder if it's all worth it. It's all of those individual pieces, one here, one there, that eat up your profits . . . and your time.

So you fill out the Assessment Chart, noting your top clients and your not-so-top clients. Since you're an online retailer with many one-and-done clients, you really don't have to "fire" any of the diseased clients. Instead, you focus on getting the Wish Lists of your top five clients. And oddly enough, even the top clients who keep buying from you still have a high rate of merchandise returns, especially when they buy your newest designs.

So, you pick up the phone and call the top five. They are thrilled to know there is a "real person" behind the business, and doubly pleased that the actual owner of the company is making the call.

During the client interview, you learn that three of your five clients operate vintage clothing stores and sell a lot of jewelry to brides looking for jewelry to wear on their big day. They all express frustration at being unable to find matching pieces for brides and bridesmaids. And online jewelry is a little bit of a necessary risk for them; a new piece may look great in a picture but when they get it and match it to the dresses, many times it doesn't work out— hence the high degree of returns. You ask, "If you had a line of costume jewelry for the bride and her attendants, would you carry it in your store?" All of your top clients respond with an eager "Yes!"

So you do some research and discover that no one is doing this. No one. You call your best designer/manufacturer and tell them about your idea—to design a line specifically for brides. You agree that your online store will be the exclusive distributor of the line, and then you go back to the top clients to bounce more ideas off them, until you're absolutely sure you know exactly what they want.

You re-brand your online store to gear it specifically to bridal boutiques and retailers. First you line up all your top clients with jewelry to stock at their stores. They only need one or two samples of each design, since they just use it to show to the dozens of brides that come through their stores each day. And when a bride likes a piece, it's the shop owner who orders it online. This is working great . . . time to expand!

You start with the people you know—those who operate small shops and vintage clothing stores—and show up everywhere they are. You're at the right trade shows and festivals and events. You place an ad in the handful of targeted trade magazines and newsletters, and on industry-related blogs. And you show up at all of the runway and trunk shows for new designs.

Soon, you have dozens of retailers carrying your lines. And, because you've moved in concentric circles within your industry, you also have new relationships with designers who ask you to collaborate on the design of a new line specifically for their own bridal attire. Your company is written up in magazines and on major bridal blogs, and soon brides from all over the country are buying jewelry directly from your website. And because you're selling an entire collection of jewelry (necklace, earrings, rings) in one shot, rather than just one piece at a time, you can generate more profit per sale . . . not to mention, you use up fewer resources (time, shipping supplies, etc.) to get them out the door.

Most importantly, you killed the costume jewelry curve and created your own, niche-specific curve within the bridal industry. Even though you now have competitors, you're the dominant player because a) you were first, b) you know this industry inside and out and c) you have fantastic relationships with designers and retailers because you *listened* and *responded* to their frustrations and wishes.

Now your business is a giant in the industry, and you're getting a full night's sleep every night. Life is sweet.

CHAPTER THREE

THE SEED

Chuck Radcliffe grows mammoth pumpkins. But he's not your typical pumpkin farmer; he's a backyard gardener who became obsessed with growing the big orange beasts the first time he tried to grow a pumpkin large enough to fit a baby inside. No, he's not a weirdo. (At least not *that* kind of weirdo.) Since his son was born on October 29th, Chuck figured he would take a picture of his newborn wrapped in a blanket, inside a pumpkin with just his head sticking out. Aww.

The following Halloween, Chuck grew a pumpkin big enough to fit his then one-year-old son inside so he could snap another pic—and he's been trying to grow bigger and bigger pumpkins for that annual photo op ever since. For him, the task became a bizarre race of who can grow faster, Chuck Jr. or Chuck's pumpkins. Sure enough, Chuck's skills kept pace, and within eighteen years he was growing pumpkins so big that they could hold, well, an eighteen-year-old *and* his hormones. Can you imagine the awkward moment when Chuck Jr. brings home his new girlfriend? If she makes it through the annual photo op, he'd better marry that girl!

When Chuck started growing giant pumpkins, he did it just to get the photos. Now, he's in it to win it—the New Jersey state record, that is. (What? Jersey? Yup. You thought we only had highways and hit men? Well, we have pumpkins, too, palsy-walsy.)

When I started writing this book I sought out pumpkin farmers who are only barely this side of strange; those people, like Chuck, for whom growing huge pumpkins is a lifestyle, an all-consuming passion. I had built two successful businesses using the same strategy they use to build giant pumpkins, so I thought, hey, what else do they know?

After an hour on the phone with Chuck I knew more about watering methods and planting formation than 99.9 percent of the population. I was fascinated. I was furiously taking notes about the varying pumpkin hardiness on the naturally forming Christmas tree–patterned root structure when he told me about Niagara Falls.

Apparently, every year Chuck and a few hundred giant-pumpkin-lovin' growers make the pilgrimage to Niagara Falls for the International Giant Vegetable Grower's Convention. (No, I'm not making this up. And no, this is not the subject of Christopher Guest's latest follow-up to *Best in Show*.)

"All of the top growers come," Chuck said. "And over a couple of beers at a bar one of them might just give you a seed worth five hundred dollars, so I figure it's worth the trip."

Hold up. A seed worth $500? He must mean a bucket of seeds . . . or at least a packet, right?

"Five hundred dollars for just one seed? Are you serious?"

"Yeah. And that's nothing. The best seeds start at around eighteen hundred dollars," Chuck explained.

I was floored. "For *one* seed," I said again.

"Yeah. One seed."

"Sorry," I said. "It just seems like a lot of money for something so small."

"Yeah, well, if you want to grow a prize-winning pumpkin, you have to plant a prize-winning pumpkin seed."

So true, Chuck. So true.

He explained that you can't grow a pumpkin the size of a car from a regular pumpkin seed. All of the growers want the spawn of car-sized pumpkins so they can grow even more car-sized pumpkins and win that blue ribbon.

And that's when Chuck told me about Howard Dill.

All of the giant pumpkins you see on the six o'clock news—no matter whether you're watching from your couch in Topeka or your recliner in St. Paul—come from the same lineage of seeds, the Dill's Atlantic Giant variety started by the godfather of giant pumpkins, the late Howard Dill of Nova Scotia, Canada.

"If you want to grow a big pumpkin, you need to plant an Atlantic seed," Chuck says. "There is no substitute."

I wanted to learn more, so as soon as I wrapped up with Chuck, I Googled "Howard Dill." I found out that Dill was a lifelong farmer and that his Dill's Atlantic Giant seeds are behind every world record since his own first win, in 1979. (He grew them on his farm near the pond where ice hockey was invented . . . how great is that?) Dill went on to patent his seeds and now they are sold to dozens of seed companies worldwide. His family took over the operation after he passed away. To pumpkin-growing enthusiasts, Dill is a legend. He was the giant of giant-pumpkin farmers. He *owned* his niche.

I couldn't stop thinking about the $1,800 pumpkin seed, so I did the math. Since a single pumpkin seed that weighs about

1/200 of an ounce can cost upwards of $1,800, you know what that means . . . giant pumpkins seeds are worth more than gold. Like *way* more than gold. Think about it. As I write this, *Forbes* reports that an ounce of gold is worth about $1,750. An ounce of prize-winning, Atlantic Giant pumpkins seeds will run you around, oh, $300,000. You can buy basic Atlantic Giant pumpkin seeds for $10 a packet, but *just a few* seeds from the prizewinners will cost more than your car.

If you haven't figured it out by now, the reason I'm telling you all this is not to get you to invest all your money in Dill's Atlantic Giant pumpkin seeds. The reason this is relevant to you is because in order to build the most successful company you possibly can, you need to start with your own Atlantic Giant seed.

When you first started your business, you, like me, probably planted a lot of different kinds of seeds. You had a ton of great ideas, welcomed every type of client with open arms and busted your butt trying to make those seeds grow. You watered, and watered . . . and watered . . . until you were drowning. Some seeds worked out better than others, growing perfectly acceptable pumpkins . . . I mean, profits. But other seeds just withered and died even after you spent precious resources you really didn't have trying to keep them alive. Other seeds just never even pushed through the soil at all.

But what if you put all of your time and energy into the most awesome, most promising, most valuable seed? This is a seed that, with your expert love and care, would surely grow a vine able to produce a pumpkin of mammoth proportions. What if you didn't have to spend time or money trying to grow a bunch of different seeds in different ways? What if you knew for sure that your seed would respond to your best efforts and grow, grow, grow?

I'm going to step in and answer for you (because as much as I'd like to hear your answer, the author–reader relationship isn't that interactive . . . yet). It's really a no-brainer. If you planted seeds worth more than one hundred and fifty times the value of gold guaranteed to grow super pumpkins large enough to supply your entire town with pumpkin pie, you'd be stoked. You'd also be happy, fulfilled and, most likely, rich.

Chuck knows he only needs one of Dill's super-special seeds to grow a whole vine of pumpkins, and that if he follows proven growing methods, he'll likely get at least one freakishly large pumpkin. If he wants more than one, he follows the same protocol, and plants another one of Dill's magic makers.

Don't waste your time planting seeds that may or may not work out. Plant the seed that you *know* has the very best chance of making it, and then focus your attention, money, time and other resources on that tight niche until all of your entrepreneurial dreams come true.

FINDING YOUR OWN GIANT SEED

The main difference between you and an aspiring giant pumpkin farmer is that you already have your best seed, you just have to find it.

Your giant seed is basically your sweet spot—the place where your best clients and the best part of your business meet. This is the place where your favorite customers are able to derive maximum benefit from the systematized, core process that drives your business.

In the next chapter I'll clue you in on how to assess your client roster and identify your best clients, but for now, just think of them as the people you most want to work with—those who give you the most business, have reasonable expectations, and communicate well. I know you have a short list of fave clients whom you prioritize without a second thought, so let's go with them for right now.

And, if you're just starting out and don't have clients, just picture your ideal client. This should be easy because your ideal clients should be a lot like you. They should share your interests, values, principles, aspirations and have a similar personality and approach to business.

In many ways your best customers are like your best friends.

They like you and you like them. Everything is easy between you because you "get" each other, you respect each other, you have fun together. Plus, you each get something great out of the relationship: they get a service they need and you get the premium they're willing to pay for it. Model your ideal client after your best friends and sure enough, everything will become easier.

Your core system is the unique offering that differentiates your business from all the others in your industry. It's not just about product or service; it's also about your approach to delivering your product or service, and it's about the specific talents, abilities and experience you bring to the table. It's your big idea, your know-how and your mojo all wrapped up into one crazy cocktail that can't be duplicated.

In *The Toilet Paper Entrepreneur* I talked about the importance of focusing on one Area of Innovation (AOI) and explained the three types: quality, price and convenience. Nobody can be the de facto leader in all three areas simultaneously. Many try, and all fail. You can't deliver premium quality super fast at rock-bottom prices. That's just not happening.

For example, we all know Wal-Mart is a price leader. Price is their game, and they win almost every time. So what happened when they tried to get into the convenience game with their own online DVD rental service, intending to compete with Netflix and Blockbuster? They didn't just lose; they bombed. In true Wal-Mart fashion, they undercut Netflix and Blockbuster's monthly fee, but in less than two years they had only 300,000 subscribers. At the time, Netflix had ten times that, with three million subscribers (Blockbuster had just over 800,000 subscribers). And, Wal-Mart did not have the infrastructure in place to compete on convenience—Netflix had more distribution centers, so they could deliver more DVDs to more people, faster than Wal-Mart. Even the mighty Wal-Mart can't compete in an area outside their core competency of cheap price. And you can't either.

You have to make a choice. What is your AOI? Are you the quality guy, who takes the time to get it right? (Think Mercedes.) Can you give clients the best price? (Think Wal-Mart.) Or can you offer exceptionally convenient service or delivery of products? (Think McDonald's.)

But wait a second. McDonald's also has the best price. A jumbo sized hamburger, fries and a soda bigger then your head, handed to you through your car window in sixty seconds for only $7.99. So there you have it: fastest and cheapest. Right?

Wrong. McDonald's isn't in the price game; McDonald's is in the *convenience* game. Last time I went to the supermarket, I could get a two-liter bottle of soda, a pound of ground chuck and a couple Idaho spuds for less than the cost of a McDonald's combo meal. You can feed a family of four for the same price! So the supermarket wins on price. But man oh man, a burger in sixty seconds flat sounds good. McDonald's dominates on convenience.

Your AOI is only one component of your unique offering; another is your number-one strength, that thing you do really, really well. It's the thing that just comes naturally to you; it's so easy to execute, it doesn't feel like work. Your number-one strength is also the thing you love most, that makes you feel all happy inside. And for all of these reasons, it's the thing you want to do *first*. You don't have to psych yourself up to do it or ask for help; it's second nature. And because you've probably been playing that jack-of-all-trades game, it's likely the thing you *miss* doing, the thing you wish you could be doing—if only you could stop doing all that other stuff.

Combine your AOI and your number-one strength with your life *and* your business experience—experience that no one else has because they're just *not you*—and you've discovered how your company is authentically different than the competition. Your unique offering is the combination of your AOI, your number-one strength and the qualities, attributes, talents and interests that make you, you.

To get to your sweet spot, you also have to take into account your ability to systematize every aspect of your business. You may think (like Eric) that your industry is too unique or nuanced to systematize, but that's not the case. As your business grows over time, it should become easier to systematize, not harder. Things will come naturally to you, you'll build more contacts and have more people on your team who know how things work. So when you consider your ability to systematize, ask yourself, "Is this easy to do today, and can I keep making it easier and easier, over time?"

Systematization is what will allow you to leave the business for a four-week vacation knowing that everything will work just fine without you. And if you do it right, your business may even grow.

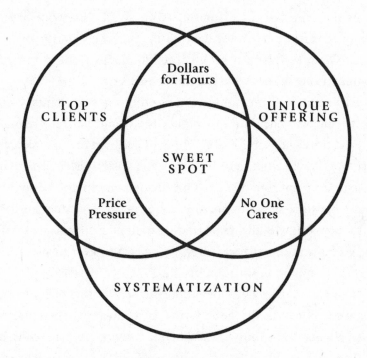

I'm a visual guy. My office walls are covered in giant white-boards and black chalkboard paint. So I drew this little diagram to help you find your seed. Look at the picture, and I'll break it down for you. I dare say, this little drawing gives Frank a run for his money.

On the top left you have your Top Clients, the individuals and businesses who, through working the Assessment Chart (see the next chapter), have risen to the top of your existing client roster—in other words, these are your best clients. On the top right we have your Unique Offering, the combination of your Area of Innovation, your number-one strength and your experience. And on the bottom we have Systematization, your ability to easily execute and replicate your offering through automation or people.

At the center of the diagram is your sweet spot, your opportunity for super growth. By definition, your sweet spot—your Atlantic Giant seed—must hit all three marks to work. Any other combination will not yield the same results.

For example, if you're only working with your best clients (you'll figure out who they are in Chapter Four) and you're offering a unique product or service (something that is hard or impossible for a competitor to duplicate) but you can't easily systematize (you have to do it yourself and can't get anyone else to do it) you'll be under constant pressure because you'll never have enough time or money. You will always be trading hours for dollars—like Eric, the globe-trotting, race car–driving guy who never turns off his phone . . . and never turns on his life.

If you're offering a unique product or service that's easy to systematize, but basically nobody wants it, meaning there are no "best clients" to be found, well, then it's obvious: you're screwed.

And, if you're working with your best clients and can easily systematize, but your offering is far from unique, there's no barrier to entry and the competition will beat you up on price . . . often . . . and in a million other ways, too. Which means you'll never grow your business into the giant we both know it can become.

Jorge Morales and Jose Pain learned this lesson the hard way. When in 2007 they first launched Specialized ECU Repair, a company focused on the repair of electronic control units (ECU) for luxury cars (the fancy-schmancy computers that, when busted, can bring a $100,000 car down in a nanosecond), helping as many clients as possible was the goal. Because a repaired ECU can last thirty years, most of their clients were one-offs. So they tried to be accommodating to all requests for repair, even for European cars with technologies they hadn't quite figured out yet.

Although both were experienced electrical engineers, they had a specialty—they could turn around ECUs for nearly every make and model of Porsche and BMW within only a few days. Other luxury brands, not so much. It wasn't that they *couldn't* fix an ECU for a Jaguar, it was just that they couldn't fix it within a week, which was their promise. Still, because Jorge and Jose wanted to grow their business, they did what most entrepreneurs do when they first start a business—they accepted jobs that they probably shouldn't have.

"We got tempted in the beginning. We wanted to see if we could repair the ECUs we were less familiar with as quickly as the ones we had mastered," Jorge explained to me. "We had to back out and refund the money they gave us to perform the repair. We had to drop a few things we weren't the best at—like very early Jaguars— because we were really hurting the clients who were putting their faith in us to get the job done."

So they narrowed their focus and only accepted jobs they *knew* they could knock out of the park. They catered to their clients, giving them quality repairs they could rely on. Over time, they got even better at repairing ECUs for Porsche and BMW. "As we got more jobs and developed more tools, our turnaround time changed dramatically. Now, we can fix five computers in an hour, and make $2,500." In an effort to systematize even further, they also adopted an ECU exchange program that allowed them to get new computers to clients overnight, in exchange for their old ECU.

Jorge and Jose found their sweet spot, that place where the needs of their best clients (fast, reliable turnaround) intersected with their unique offering (AOI = quality; number-one strength = Porsche and BMW) and systematization (new tools and programs designed to streamline process).

"When we tried to do too much, we didn't make as much money. Now, we are just servicing ECUs for Porsche and BMW. It doesn't make much sense why we are making more money by focusing [so narrowly]. But it's true." So true.

To grow your business you need to zero in on that sweet spot that covers all three components, not just one or two. Otherwise you'll just be running around watering all the different seeds, but not the Atlantic Giant. And if you don't plant the Atlantic Giant—even if the other seeds do take root—it will never be a giant. You'll end up watering and caring for it forever, and still end up with a four-pounder. We already know where that strategy leads. Do I need to remind you of the drooling, one-nut guy? He's probably sitting on your shoulder. (Don't look, don't look! He gets mean when you look directly at him.) Well, kick him off right now, because you know he never even *heard* of a sweet spot.

THERE'S ONLY ONE ATLANTIC GIANT

A lot of people get into business and immediately try to copy the other guy. This is human nature. In grade school we want to have the same toys the other kids have, watch the same cartoons, root for the same sports teams. In high school we try to fit in with the popular clique by copying their style, their slang and even their beliefs and values. As adults, we try to keep up with the people we admire—driving the same type of car, going on the same vacations, buying the same crap.

We constantly look at other people and base our decisions on how we can be better or how we can be more like them. What's the very first thing you did when it was time to design a website for your company? I bet you looked at a few of your competitors' sites. How about when you ran a "help wanted" ad to hire your first employee? I bet you copied the ad your biggest competitor was running (and probably downloaded their legal agreements off their site, too).

What about when you launched a new product? Did you check out what the competition had to offer before you developed your own? I bet you did. No shame or blame—I've done it myself. But it is a trap. It is a trap because you can't find your Atlantic Giant seed in someone else's patch. You can't create a copy of the Atlantic Giant seed; you need your own. You can continue learning from others, including the competition, but to find your sweet spot, you need to be yourself.

While you do have to stay up on what the competition is doing, you also need to understand they don't have your Atlantic Giant seed. Shoot, if anything, they represent more weeds encroaching on your patch. All of this comparing and judging and trying to catch up with them is a huge mistake, because it keeps you away from the sweet spot. When you stop looking at the other guy and start focusing on how you can easily offer something truly unique, something your best customers really want; when you do what's easiest, what's the most fun, what satisfies you the most; you stop being a follower in competition with everyone else. You become a leader.

In the words of the great amateur pumpkin farmer Chuck Radcliffe, "If you want to grow a prize-winning pumpkin, you have to plant a prize-winning pumpkin seed." There's only one Atlantic Giant in your patch, and you don't have to drive to Niagara Falls to get it. You just have to work the plan, man. Just work the plan.

Work the plan—
Take Action in 30 minutes (or Less)

1. *Start the chart.* In the next section you are going to discover who your best clients are, but first you need to put the groundwork in place. Draw and label three circles on piece of paper. Or, you can download some pre-drawn circles at www.PumpkinPlan.info. Hang it in a place where you will see it every day, and start filling in the details as you discover them. This is not a one-shot. Be prepared to review, tweak and improve often.

2. *Zero in on your Area of Innovation (AOI).* What's your "thing"? What is your company known for? Is it speedy delivery or fast response times? Do you have a commitment to excellence that is unparalleled in your industry? Or are you the cheapest date around? Take a few minutes to figure out your AOI. And remember, you can't be all things to all people. You can only be *one* thing to a group of important people—your best clients. Where do you *really* innovate— quality, speed/efficiency or price? Now that you know where you innovate, answer this question: How could you take this AOI to a level of innovation that is rarely, or better yet, *never* seen in the industry?

3. *Figure out if you can systematize it.* What tasks do you handle yourself because you think that's easier than teaching someone else how to do them? What are the tasks that, if you went on a four-week vacation, would not get done? If you took a break, would your business fall apart at the seams? Make a list of all these things, because these are the places where you need to start creating systems. Building a system is painful and it takes time, maybe ten times, maybe one hundred times longer than "just doing it." But when the system is done and in place, it becomes automatic and you will never, ever need to do it again.

How to Pumpkin Plan Your Industry — Construction

Let's pretend you're a general contractor. Get out your overalls, your big black dented lunch box and your 1970s Tyco hammer—we are about to Pumpkin Plan the construction industry.

You're a general contractor—you facilitate the building of homes and other buildings—in a challenging market, competing for the same customers as all of the other contractors: the developers catering to young families, the developers catering to retirees, the developers catering to single professionals, and so on. Like everyone else, you're also trying to snatch up referrals from architects who hook you up with individual clients—all kinds, even those who are totally bonkers. In a down market—heck, in *any* market—you'll take what you can get.

After filling out your Assessment Chart you know exactly which clients need to go—the guy who seems to have a 240-day-net payment policy, the developer who drags out jobs and then changes deadlines at a moment's notice. It's easy to cut them loose because just the thought of not having to deal with them makes you want to skip down the street like Mary freaking Poppins. You simply tell Late-pay Larry you're raising your prices and implementing a hefty finance-charge policy. Larry's smart, so he's off to find someone else who will float him. And Team Procrastination? You fire them by instituting another policy change: fees for delaying the project *and* rush fees. They're out of there.

With your two biggest diseased clients gone, you can start trimming the fat. Now that you aren't chasing Larry down for payment, do you really need a full-time bookkeeper? Could you get by with a part-time bookkeeper? Could you cut back on your work force?

Next, you focus on how you can nurture your top clients: developers. Before you reach out to them, notice what they have in common, if anything. Do they specialize in green building? Do they market to a specific demographic? Do they require specific building materials? By looking at their similarities, you can begin to form a plan that will cater specifically to developers.

You call the six top clients and ask for a meeting to discuss how you could serve them better. "What are your biggest gripes about *our* construction industry?" "If you could ask for anything and get it, what do you wish general contractors like us would do for developers like you?" "What would make your experience (life *and* business) *easier, better, more profitable?*"

After you get a few wish lists, you notice that two developers really want homebuilders who can work fast, like lightning fast. It seems there's a market for speedy home construction. You've built a few homes in record time before, and it was actually pretty lucrative. And, you can develop systems so that it's pretty darn easy to turn these projects around, one right after the other. Between the rush fees and the "no-time-to-change-your-mind" policy, you actually end up making more money building homes super fast. Huh. Why didn't you realize this earlier? (Hint: because you were too busy building everything from dog houses to McMansions . . . and your bookkeeper had her hands full trying to get Larry to pay up!)

Suddenly you've hit the sweet spot—that magic place where

your top clients and your most lucrative service intersect with the ability to systematize. What if you specialize in super speedy construction? You know for a fact that none of your many competitors bill themselves as such, so if you zero in on this specialized service, you'd be the go-to guy. The *authority*.

So you start shifting your focus, fulfilling existing contracts but restructuring your business around your new niche. You go back to your top clients and tell them, "Hey, you said you wanted fast construction, and we're thinking of specializing in this. Here's our plan—could you give me some honest feedback?" You take note, adjusting your strategy until they jump at the chance to get on your schedule.

Even with this new focus and capability, many prospects and clients still call you the "builder guy." So you give yourself a new label. You are now a provider of "rapid residential construction services." "What is that?" your customers ask. Perfect. You have opened up the opportunity to tell them your differences.

Now, you have *loads* of lucrative projects from your top clients, who totally love you because you gave them their wish. Their business is booming. Your business is booming. So you go back to your top clients, the developers, and ask, "Would you refer me to your preferred vendors? I'd like to brainstorm with them to figure out how we can make your life even easier, better, more awesome." Now, you're a rock star. Better yet, you're about to rev up the vendor referral engine.

You meet with insurance brokers, mortgage lenders, architects. They dig you because you just want to help them out, and you band together to make your mutual clients happy. So when someone asks them, "Do you know any builders who can put up a quality house in less than six weeks?" they say, "Heck, yeah. I know a great guy who *specializes* in rapid residential construction. Let me hook you up." Notice that? The other vendors are using your label. Nicely done.

Soon, yours is the *only* company people go to when they need a house, fast. You're the biggest pumpkin around. Down market? What's that? Your business no longer depends on interest rates, trends or even beating the competition. There *is* no competition. Someone will always need a rush build. Always.

CHAPTER FOUR

ASSESS THE VINE

As emphatic as I've been up to now, and as many times as I've promised you that the Pumpkin Plan works, I know you're probably still thinking "This guy's a loonbag. No way am I cutting clients!" (Or some version of that.) Even if you believe I *might* be on to something, you probably think, like Bruce the wedding florist, that continuing to work like a dog will eventually pay off. (It *has* to, right?) Sure, you'll cut your class-A creeps, but you're not going to cut *all* the clients who make you miserable or cost you money. What if it backfires? What if one of those clients gets his act together right after you cut him off? What if you end up with just a handful of clients?

More is not better, people. *Better* is better.

You need to shift your mindset away from the quantity game. You need to stop killing yourself for scraps. I want you to kick your fears in the teeth and start focusing on the clients who, when you

love them (and others just like them), will make your wildest revenue dreams possible.

When my pal AJ Harper started her freelance writing business
in 2005, she said yes to every job she could get. She wrote articles,
books, blog posts—anything and everything. And I do mean
anything. She'll probably kill me for telling you this, but she once
took a job writing articles about penis enlargement for a quasi-
pharmaceutical distributor. And, no, the stuff does not work. Do
not ask me how I know this.

The thing was, even though she made enough to live on, she
wasn't making it, not really. She worked seven days a week and
still ended up borrowing money from her folks to get by. Worse,
she spent hours every day bidding on new projects, trying to get
new clients.

Fast-forward six years, and she's making it. She's got a team
working under her, and together they turn out book after amazing
book for her company, Book Lab. The other day we were chatting
over chili dogs and root beer. She explained how she started to
turn things around. "A couple of years in, I realized I had a handful of clients I loved working with, and they all had a few things
in common," she said. "They all had the goods, meaning they
weren't a bunch of blowhards with empty promises for readers.
They all had the stamina and the will to get their books out into
the world. And most importantly, they respected me, which meant
we could collaborate—and that's what I love best."

So she focused on her better clients and stopped trying to get
more clients. Within a matter of months, new prospects started
calling her after being referred by her top clients. And because she
had new qualifiers for clients (have the goods, have stamina, have
respect), she said yes only to those who fit and no to those who
didn't. She hasn't bid on a project or marketed her business in any

way since 2007. Clients just show up, clients she loves just as much as the handful of *better* clients who inspired her to set new standards. She isn't borrowing money from the folks, either. If anything, they are borrowing from her.

More isn't better. *Better* is better.

THE DESERT ISLAND QUESTION

There are three types of clients, and their importance is ranked exactly as follows: 1. good clients, 2. non-existent clients, and 3. bad clients. Looking at that list, you may want to rearrange the order, maybe move "non-existent clients" to the end, because having bad clients is better than having no clients at all, right? Nope. Just like bad, rotten pumpkins suck nutrients from good pumpkins and stunt their growth, bad, rotten clients distract you, drain your resources and cost you money. You're much better off having no clients than bad clients, because at least when you don't have any clients you can prospect for good ones instead of tailoring, tweaking and twisting to accommodate the needs of the bad ones.

Which brings me to my next question. You've probably answered the "desert island" question many times in the course of your life. You know, the one that goes something like this: "If you were trapped on a desert island and could only bring one of (fill in the blank of each type of thing: toiletry, person, playlist, etc.) what would it be?" Me? I'm going with a toothbrush, a Navy Seal and the greatest hairband album of all time, Def Leppard's *Pyromania*.

Before you get up in my face, there's a reason I picked a Navy Seal over my loving, gorgeous, awesome wife (she may read this, you know). I didn't pick her because if we *were* stranded on a desert island together, we'd be dead in less than two hours. Seriously, we are two of the most mechanically challenged people on the planet. Add to that the fact that I faint at the sight of blood, she has a sun allergy, and we may or may not have gotten lost *inside* a Sandals resort once: we were five minutes away from needing a helicopter rescue . . . from the pool. My wife and I have enough ineptitude to ensure our certain (and likely, painful) death. So I pick the Navy Seal. Those guys can do *anything*.

Here's my desert island question for you: If you could only bring one client to a desert island, who would it be? Who could you stand to be with for the months or years it takes you to figure out how to get off the island? Who can you trust? Who do you love? Who might actually work with you to find the way to survive—or even thrive—during your stay?

When figuring out which clients deserve VIP status, you can't just go with revenue, and you can't just go with your gut. If you truly want to pull off this whole entrepreneur thing, you're going to need awesome clients you really connect with, clients who make you want to go to work in the morning, not hide under the covers. You want clients who have potential, who are open to new ideas, who have the money to pay you what you're worth, who respect you, who are going places and who want you to be part of it. You can't leave finding those awesome clients to fate. And you most certainly can't wait for your awful clients to suddenly realize how great you are and turn into awesome ones. That never happens. N to the E to the V to the E to the R. Never.

So how do you take control over your client list? First, identify your ideal client, your "desert island" client, the most promising pumpkin on the vine. Then, keep your eyes peeled for the clones, those clients who are so much like that other rock-star pumpkin, you can barely tell them apart. Why is this so important? Because you need the best, most promising clients to grow your business—and lots of 'em. Duh, Michelob-shits. (That was one of the wonderful nicknames my high school friends gave me.)

"But, Mike," you say. "Can't you have a bunch of awesome clients who are awesome in their own way?"

No. You can't.

Here's why. Obviously you can't build a business on one client, no matter how great he or she is, since that would make you wholly dependent on their success. But you also can't effectively create systems for one hundred completely different customers. If you can't systematize, you can't scale your business. And if you can't scale your business, you'll be stuck on the hamster wheel forever.

So who's going to go all *Survivor: Get Me Off this Island* with you? Who is your number one, all-time, absolute favorite client? More importantly, *why* did you choose this client? Her mad hunting skills? His ability to make a radio out of two coconuts and some seaweed? Their wicked funny stories? It's vital that you understand why you like working with your top client, why they're good for business and why they make your life easier, so that you can first identify which of your other clients have at least some of those qualities, and then later, spot new clients who have *most* of those qualities.

If you can't even think of one existing client you would be willing to be stranded with, conjure one up. Create your own dream client (like Frankenstein, but smarter) by blending the best parts of your ho-hum clients—the great communication from one combined with the lighting-fast payments of another. What qualities would this assembled top client have? Prestigious connections? Vast resources? The willingness to forgive you when you stumble? I know stitching up awesome clients can feel strange when it wasn't so long ago (maybe yesterday) that you were practically begging for clients, *any* clients. But remember, you're going to clone this Franko-client over and over again; shouldn't you clone the best?

THE ASSESSMENT CHART

Obviously you can't fire all but one of your clients. You've got to eat. So how do you figure out who goes and who stays? Like every little step in this plan, it's pretty simple. (And this step even has a handy-dandy chart!)

When I started implementing the Pumpkin Plan in my first business, I followed Frank's advice about how to rank clients—first by revenue earned, then by cringe factor. But over time I developed my own, more comprehensive (sorry, Frank) method for ranking them, and gave it a sophisticated, clever name. Are you ready for it? I called it . . . drum roll . . . the Assessment Chart. Yeah, okay. Not clever. But who has time for clever when your nuts are on the line?

When it comes to rating clients or customers, there are some pretty basic qualifiers that apply to all businesses. Do they pay on time, when they feel like it or not at all? Do they refer others to you, or do they keep you all to themselves? Would they tell you if you made a horrible (or horribly stupid) mistake, let you fix it and let it go, or would they rub your nose in it every chance they got? Is a super-sweet deal on the horizon, or are they maxed out with you? Do they tell you what they need and want, or do they expect you to read their minds? Do they respect your expertise, or do they consistently undermine or question you? Are they coming back for more, more, more, or are they one-hit wonders?

You also have your own qualifiers—the qualities you look for in a shipwreck buddy (top client). Maybe you're looking for clients who prefer a specific product or service you provide. You know where you make your money—wouldn't it be fantastic if *all* of your clients bought that product or used that service?

You can make your own Assessment Chart, or you can go online and download the one I made for you at www.PumpkinPlan .info. I've included all of the basic qualifiers, and space for you to add your own. Here's how you make it:

1. List your clients in descending order of revenue.

2. Now, put a line through the clients who make you cringe when you hear their names.

3. Create a column for each of the following qualifiers:

> *Pays Fast*—do they pay on time, or early?

> *Repeat Revenue*—do they use your services or purchase from you on a regular basis?

> *Revenue Potential*—could they generate a significant amount of revenue for you in the future?

> *Communication*—do they communicate well with you?

> *Fix It*—when you make a mistake, will they tell you, give you a chance to fix it and forgive you when you do?

4. Grade each client in each column. A = perfect, B = near perfect, but messes up occasionally, C = average, D = poor, rarely meets expectations, F = completely sucks. Be honest—don't give them more credit than they're due. This is your livelihood, man, your dream. Don't worry about hurt feelings. You can keep this Assessment Chart under lock and key if you have to, but *be honest*.

5. Now create new columns for the following, less crucial qualifiers:

> *Opportunity*—does working with them give you opportunities you wouldn't have had otherwise, such as introductions to key partners?

> *Referrals*—do they refer others to you and/or are they willing to?

> *History*—do you have a long-established history working with this client, making you feel confident you understand how they behave in all situations?

6. Add blank columns for any additional qualifiers you came up with.

7. Place a "Y" (yes) or "N" (no) in each of the non-crucial columns. Use this as a tiebreaker when identifying top clients. For example, if you have two clients who both score a B on the crucial rating scale, find out which of these clients has more Ys than Ns in your non-crucial columns.

8. Add three more blank columns for your Immutable Laws (we'll fill them in later).

If you sell products to hundreds of customers, go with the top five, ten or twenty percent of your clientele (based on who brings in the most dough). Remember, customers are really clients. If you can't name your top revenue generators, jot down the names of the people you see most often. If you don't know their names (and come on, you *have* to get to know them), write down their attributes—lady with pink hair, tattoo guy, high-pitched voice—and then vow to introduce yourself at your earliest opportunity.

One common mistake entrepreneurs make when assessing clients is to unconsciously tweak their answers to key questions in order to play favorites. For whatever reason, you may want to keep a client who really needs to go, and so you overlook the negative and exaggerate the positive. Maybe it's your first client, or a relative, or a company you like being associated with. Because your heart wants to continue working with them, you look for evidence to support the idea that they are a top client and worthy of your time and attention. The fix for this is to have a third party look over your Assessment Chart, someone who knows your business and your clients, but who does *not* share your agenda or your preconceived notions. They'll make you stay real.

By now you should have a clear picture of the clients who are awesome and those who are anything but. You know the cringe-worthy clients are on their way out, but now you also know which seemingly decent clients just aren't measuring up. Surprised? Nervous? Relax. I know you aren't ready to break up with them just yet. You thought you had a good thing going and you want to see if you can work things out. I get that. We're not going to start firing until the next chapter, anyway, so for now just exhale and finish the chart.

I GET YOU

In *The Toilet Paper Entrepreneur* I wrote about Immutable Laws, the unbreakable rules you follow that serve as the spine of your business. In the same way your body's movement is compromised when your spine is out of alignment, you can't grow a healthy business when you are operating out of alignment with your Immutable Laws.

Some people refer to Immutable Laws as core values, but that just sounds too "special" to me, too malleable. Don't get me wrong; values are important. But when we think of values, we put them in the context of a specific group, like Americans, or Catholics, or Yankee fans. (Okay, maybe that last one is a stretch . . . what values do Yankees fans have? I kid. I kid.) Immutable Laws are about you, and only you. They're what *you* live by. Our values can change over time, but we don't mess with Immutable Laws. They are set in stone. They are the essence of who you are. And your business *must* adhere to them.

I have several Immutable Laws, but the two that people seem to remember the most are "Give to Give" (give for the sake of giving and work for the joy of working) and "No Dicks Allowed" (life's too short for rude, arrogant people who are only out for numero uno). I abide by these Laws at all costs. I don't deal with give-because-they-want-to-get people and I never do business with a dick.

I had a recent run-in with a dick. A dickette, to be exact. My Immutable Law spidey senses started tingling the second I overheard her treating one of her own employees like crap. While she represented a big ongoing project, she represented a much bigger headache. I quickly wrapped up my work with her and weeded her out of my pumpkin patch. I wasn't surprised that she was a dick about the breakup. Moral of the story: Just like habits, Immutable Laws are unchanging—even the bad ones. Giving people are always giving. Positive people are always positive. And dicks are, well, always dicks.

The third of my Immutable Laws is "Blood Money." Money is

the lifeblood of my business, so I'm taking my profit first and I'm not spending one unnecessary penny. As I write this I'm sitting in an office furnished for next to nothing. My whiteboard is hand-made, the desks don't match each other and my conference room looks like it hasn't been updated since 1979. But I'm cool with it. Actually I'm *more* than cool with it because that's who I am. And I'm cool with it because "Blood Money" is one of my Immutable Laws. I don't hide it. I don't pretend to have a nicer office than I do. I'm proud to be a frugal entrepreneur, so buying expensive furniture would not be my thing. It wouldn't feel right. It goes against the essence of who I am as an entrepreneur. But I'm not cheap—I'm frugal. I don't drive a junker—my car is certified pre-owned (from this century), and so is my stuff.

"Give to Give," "No Dicks Allowed" and "Blood Money" influence every decision I make. The furniture I buy. The employees I bring on board. The vendors I use. The things about me other people may call quirky become the essence of my company. When I adhere to my Immutable Laws in all aspects of business, everything flows very easily. My vendors know how to serve me best, I understand my employees and they understand me, and my clients love my style. We could all survive quite nicely on a desert island, spearin' fish and makin' music with found objects . . . or whatever castaways do with their free time. My low-grade clients—the ones who want me to break my Immutable Laws—just bitch and complain about being lost at sea, while Navy Seal Tom (yeah, I named him) plays the bongos, makes me an electric guitar out of a pineapple and whips up some killer *mojitos*—par-tay!

These Immutable Laws are mine. You may have different Immutable Laws, and if you don't, you should discover your own ASAP. How do you know what your Immutable Laws are? The easiest way is to listen to your emotions, since your emotions are the enforcers of your Immutable Laws. You know you've broken one of your Immutable Laws when you do something, and then kick yourself so hard for doing it you've got a bruise the size of Texas on your bum. You can check out other entrepreneurs' Immutable Laws, and submit your own, at www.PumpkinPlan.info.

YOUR BEST CUSTOMERS SHARE YOUR IMMUTABLE LAWS

Most entrepreneurs assume that the clients who bring in the most revenue will serve them best. The problem is that revenue alone doesn't take into account the costs you incur. Of course financial costs matter, but you also want to consider emotional costs and, in some cases, the physical costs of doing business with someone. The best way to do this is to figure out if someone shares the same Immutable Laws as you.

For example, if I try to do business with a company that follows an Immutable Law like "Look the Part," I may end up doing work for them that is inconsistent with my Immutable Law, "Blood Money." Sure, I may enjoy hanging out in their pimped-out office, playing video games on their giant flat-screen television, but we would not be a good fit professionally. My natural tendency may be to offer the "industrial" solution: long-lasting, powerful and cost effective. Yet they will probably want the flashy piece, or the expensive one, because they want to "Look the Part." This doesn't mean they're a bad person or that they're doing something wrong. But it does mean we're not compatible.

If I break my rule, I have to pretend to be something I'm not for the rest of my relationship with them, and that's impossible. We're going to hit an impasse one day, or I'll (unintentionally) mess up, because we don't fit. I'll misunderstand their instructions, or I'll become so frustrated with them that the work and the relationship will suffer. It's inevitable. Like when you start to date someone and pretend to love the same books she does. Not only will she eventually catch you in the lie, but you'll end up becoming an honorary member of the Sisterhood of the Traveling Pants Club—not what you signed up for.

Do you see how your Immutable Laws translate to expectation? If your Immutable Laws are not congruent with those of your clients, expectations aren't met. Not theirs. Not yours. Confusion sets in and costs grow exponentially. People get frustrated, then angry and finally the situation becomes a joy-sucking distraction that keeps you up at night way past the Late, Late Show.

It's simple: when you make decisions out of alignment with your Immutable Laws, you lose money. Lots of it. And if you don't know what your Immutable Laws are, I can promise you that you are losing money right now. Right this very second. Hang on . . . you just lost some more money. And a little bit more, and . . . wait for it . . . wait for it . . . that's another dollar down the drain.

Immutable Laws are critical in qualifying a customer. Now that you've figured out what yours are, you should add at least three of them to your Assessment Chart. Then, look for patterns in a client's behavior to see if they live by the same code. It's easy for me to tell if one of my clients adheres to "No Dicks Allowed" because if they don't, they'll engage in behavior that is downright dick-ish. Easy enough.

When your customer is just like you, they will be stoked with whatever you do. But they don't have to be your exact mirror image. I mean, could you imagine marrying yourself? Kind of boring. And the sex? That's just bizarre. With the customer, you just have to be close enough that you can finish each other's sentences. Your top clients are those who have the most overlay in terms of Immutable Laws. And you know what they're going to do for you down the road? Introduce you to their twins. If you surround yourself with people who get you, they will send you *more* people who get you, and pretty soon the rotten, abusive takers won't even grace your doorstep.

Those who are most in conflict with your Immutable Laws should be weeded out first. These diseased pumpkins will retard your business growth because you'll have to modify the way you naturally do things just to keep them from bailing. And if you veer off from who you really are and become an artificial form of what you *think* people want, you're just going to be a stunted, exhausted, broke-ass mess. And I think you already know what I'm talking about.

Here's the dealio: You want people to like you. I get that. It's human nature to want people to like you. But here is what you really want: you want people *like* you, to like you. That is what you should strive for. After all, as the late and so freakin' great George Carlin once said, "Anyone who drives slower than you is an idiot, and everyone who drives faster is a maniac." So just focus on forging relationships with the people who are going just your speed.

For many entrepreneurs, the endgame is freedom of expression. You say to yourself, "Someday, when I'm making X amount of money, I'll be able to do whatever I want." You'll be able to stop taking jobs from jerkwads and start doing it *your* way. You'll be choosy about the types of projects you work on and the people you want to collaborate with. You'll demand respect, and turn away work if someone isn't feeling it.

Well. That's a someday that will never come if you don't follow your Immutable Laws.

Your Immutable Laws are the solid, healthy root system that will grow giant, mongo pumpkins every time. Dare to be exactly who you are. Let your business be an amplification of your authentic self, and watch it grow by leaps and bounds.

Loads of clients

At the risk of confusing the hell out of you, I'd like to point out that having loads of clients is a very, very good thing. "Better is better" doesn't mean put a cap on the number of clients you can have, and it doesn't mean you shouldn't go after more clients. "Better is better" means be selective. Choose to work with your top clients, and then go out and get a bunch more just like them. I guess you could say, "More better is more better."

This is good news because you're going to answer the Desert Island question differently tomorrow, and next week, and the week after that. One day you'll say, "Hey, I love Maggie. I pick Maggie. She's always sending me clients . . . and brownies. Maybe she could whip up something tasty on the island. Maybe not brownies, but whatever. Yeah, I'll pick Maggie."

Then the next week, you think you'd like to take Barry. "He's super friendly, and does a ton of work with me, and he's got that whole nerdy, computer savant thing going for him, so he could probably, I don't know, whip us up a rocket or a lawn mower or something. 'Course, who needs a lawn mower on a desert island? But still, he could probably be pretty useful. So I'm going with Barry."

The very next day, when Tom the Navy Seal stops by to say "Hey" (yes, you can have Tom . . . you know you want him), you think, "Tom is the best dude ever! I *have* to pick Tom. How could I not pick Tom? That whole pineapple guitar thing he did for Michalowicz? He's multitalented!"

If you're struggling to narrow it down to one client, choose three, or five. Make it a party on the island. Client relationships are a bit like marriage. Even in a healthy marriage, you don't think your spouse is perfect every day, but you love him or her anyway. The beautiful part of business is, you can finally play out your fantasy and marry different people . . . and the feds won't burn down your compound.

You might actually need loads of clients. Maybe you sell an inexpensive product and you need a ton of clients to make it work. Maybe most people use your product or service once in a lifetime. Maybe you don't have clients, but scads of customers who, thanks to the miracle of technology, you've never met. Is there a special rule for you? No, not really. If you want to stop the madness (and the stink of desperation), you still have to figure out who your top clients are and cater to them *exclusively.*

So how do you do that when you need (or have . . . congratulations) thousands of clients, or more? It's easy. Focus on types of customers rather than actual clients, and assess each demographic as you would a specific client. Even if you only have two groups at the outset and end up killing one of the groups after you assess your vine, the solid group you have left is going to lead to one giant mother of a pumpkin.

David Hauser has one of those. His company, Grasshopper, is one of the top two, if not *the* top, providers of virtual phone systems, which allow entrepreneurs to get by without a receptionist *or* an expensive in-house phone system. When I called him up to pick his brain about how to select your best customers, he explained that when he and co-founder Siamak Taghaddos launched Grasshopper, they initially cast a pretty wide net, marketing to both small businesses and entrepreneurs.

"It's a small difference, but it was more about self-classification than type of business," he explained. Grasshopper had good numbers, but they wanted *great* numbers, and so they took a closer look at their customer base. They found that those who self-identified as entrepreneurs stayed on as customers longer than those who self-identified as small-business owners, and it cost less to provide tech support to the entrepreneurs, who seemed to be more technologically savvy.

"We tried messaging geared toward entrepreneurs, which made sense for us because that is who we knew best," David said, explaining how they narrowed down their client pool. David and his crew are serial entrepreneurs, so marketing to other entrepreneurs was a snap—they were basically marketing to themselves.

Hold on. Did you get that? They basically marketed to *themselves*. When you're working with clients who are your mirror image (or darn close), marketing is cake. "We did A/B split testing later that showed that the entrepreneurial messaging converted better [than messaging geared toward small businesses]. The more we talked about the entrepreneurial story, the better our conversion rates."

So Grasshopper ended up with more of the type of customers they really wanted—quickly expanding businesses with multiple locations—and fewer of the mom-and-pop dry cleaners who needed lots of hand-holding. Ironically (or perhaps not so ironically), they still retained tons of the clients who self-identified as small businesses because these aspired to be more like entrepreneurs and wanted to associate with a company that had an entrepreneurial message. "The idea of being an entrepreneur was more inspirational for them than being a small business owner," David explained.

I asked David how this shift in focus and messaging helped the business in other ways. "The things we were doing for our customers, the functions or features we would add for our service, were geared toward a much more focused group of people. We were able to enhance our offering for what this group wanted, and we didn't waste time fixing things they didn't care about."

David then told me the voice-to-text story, which is a great example of how focusing on top clients or top demographic groups helps you kick ass when you decide to expand and launch a new product. "We wanted to add voice-to-text transcription for voicemails. Other people in the market said the transcription needed to be perfect. But that's not what an entrepreneur cares about. They don't need perfection; they just want the gist of the message." Because they were focused on entrepreneurs exclusively, Grasshopper was able to transcribe using 100 percent automation and offer voice-to-text transcription at a fraction of the cost. And their best customers *loved* it! Others—not so much.

But despite having to give up some of their old customers, Grasshopper has served over one hundred thousand entrepreneurs since its inception in 2003. Not bad. Not bad at all.

Not a Popularity Contest

It's entirely possible you're still holding out on me. You could be thinking, "Okay, I'll fire a handful of the really sucky clients, but

I can't just get rid of the clients who don't score well on my Assessment Chart."

Umm . . . yes, you can. And you must.

Maybe not today, or tomorrow, but soon. Every time you clean house, you make room for new, better clients.

Sometimes you have to take one step back to take two steps forward. I was in Las Vegas recently, delivering a keynote for the Public Relations Society of America. A woman named Abbie introduced herself to me after my speech, and started sharing her frustrations. Like Bruce, Eric, me and you (yeah, I'm talking to you), Abbie felt trapped, tired and tapped out. She said, "I had to turn down a $15,000 a month client because I'm just swamped with my $2,000 a month clients." I said nothing. I just stared at her. She looked confused, and said, "What do you mean?" I kept staring. She still looked confused (and maybe a little irritated) and said, "I can't service the $15,000 client." Again, I said nothing, just stared. Then I saw recognition in her eyes, and she said, "Okay, I get it" and walked away.

So you and I don't need to have our own awkward stare down moment, let me be clear. You don't have to fire *everyone* who doesn't make it to the top of your list. You just have to fire those who are at the very bottom, those who are making it really, really difficult for you to take on your own $15,000 clients (or the equivalent). The clients who are hanging out in the middle with perfectly respectable, average grades can stay on. They just can't get your undivided attention right now. As you work the plan you might be surprised at who responds to the changes at your company and moves up the ranks, securing their own spot as a top client.

Business is not a popularity contest. Don't worry about having the *most* clients. Build a business that caters to the *best* clients . . .

the clients who are the best fit for *you*. You don't need to be the prom queen; you want a core group of steadfast, amazing friends who would do anything for you, and you, anything for them. Be consistent with who you are, and never compromise. When everything is in alignment with your basic qualifiers and your Immutable Laws—including your client roster—new, like-minded, *awesome* clients will flock to you. They'll hear about you, read about you, stumble upon you and say, "Oh, I love him. I love her! I know him. I know her!"

More is not better. *Better* is better.

Work the Plan—
Take Action in 30 Minutes (or Less)

1. *Declare your Immutable Laws.* If you haven't identified and declared your Immutable Laws, do so now. What do you stand for? Where do you draw the line? What do you absolutely have to have in place in order to connect with someone? Refine it to the core three or four Immutable Laws. Write them down, post them everywhere (including your website), tell everyone. Check out www.PumpkinPlan.info for ideas.

2. *Finish the Assessment Chart.* I know you didn't actually work the chart while you were reading the chapter, so do it now. You can draw up your own, or go to www.PumpkinPlan.info to download an Assessment Chart you can simply fill in. Depending on how many clients you have, this may take longer than thirty minutes, but do it now, anyway. Your success depends on it. The Pumpkin Plan is not just a theory; it actually works. So finish up and then let's get down to business.

How to Pumpkin Plan Your Industry — Finance

Let's pretend you're a freelance financial planner, out to fight the good fight and give people the straight scoop about retirement, insurance and all of that other sexy stuff. Get out your calculator, sharpen your no. 2 pencil and put on your trifocals—we're going to Pumpkin Plan your industry.

You have a small office—it's just you and Elaine, your administrative assistant, occupying the four rooms (plus half-bathroom) in the modest "office park" outside of town. You have a nice waiting room and conference room, but you rarely use them. You have a handful of clients, but you're struggling to make ends meet. Times are hard, and most people are just trying to keep their heads above water. Most of them aren't even *thinking* about financial planning, and those who are go straight to your biggest competitors first (bigger offices, nicer logo, stronger advertising).

So you get out your Assessment Chart and start calling the top clients on your list. You ask, "Could I come over and meet with you to get a sense of how I could serve you better? It's not a sales call; I'd just like to get your thoughts about my industry as a whole." Almost everyone agrees, so you set up a series of interviews with your best clients, in their homes, in their offices, at Starbucks—wherever they want to meet. You do this because, well, you've always done this. You're kind of the country doctor of financial planning—you make house calls. This isn't entirely unusual; insurance agents do it all the time. But you've shown up at your clients' kids' baseball games, in hotel rooms (don't ask), at the local bar.

And as it turns out, that's what your clients like most about you—that you're willing to meet them on their own turf, whenever and wherever. That you're so flexible and accommodating, and therefore, less intimidating. And that's what you love most about your job, too. You love working with people in their own environment, getting to know them in their kitchens, at the gym, in their break rooms at work. They love that you know them intimately, and that you not only can rattle off their kids' names and birthdays, but that you know how many payments they have left on their new Volvo and how much they are paying the home health aide caring for their mom. You're good on your feet; this is where you figure out who they really are and what they really need.

In the interview process you discover that at least half of your top clients wish you had more advice for them about dealing with debt, and about how to navigate life's downturns. Some of them complain that financial planners are always talking about the future, when clients can't see past covering next month's mortgage payment. The future is too abstract, and they don't want to think about how they're failing in two dimensions at the same time— right now, and in the future.

So you get this idea. What if you combined the best thing about you with the thing they want most, and truly differentiate yourself from your competition? What if you do this crazy thing that actually suits you perfectly? What if you become the financial resuscitator? Kind of like a superhero, except you don't bend steel or set things on fire with your mind. But you show up on their doorstep with a killer strategic plan that will help them dig themselves out of whatever crisis prompted them to call you. You pump life (aka financial freedom) back into people.

After you tweak your idea and run it by Elaine and your top

clients, you decide to go for it. You buy a van, have your new logo painted on it, and give up your office. (Elaine can work from home, which she really wanted, anyway.) Now you've saved thousands in rent, utility, insurance and parking expenses.

You start writing free articles and columns for the local newspaper, for newsletters and websites focused on helping people get out of debt or deal with bankruptcy or other financial crises. You set up a "financial resuscitation day" at your church (or town hall, or library) every two months, where you offer free advice to people all day long. You take out a few ads—nothing major, but always with the picture of your van and "Bringing you financial stability today, giving you financial freedom tomorrow!" as your tagline.

Before, people simply called you the "financial planning guy," just like all of your competitors. Now you are known as a "financial resuscitator" and your phone is ringing off the hook. You're so good at saving people money that you simply charge a percentage of the savings for your "resuscitation" service—meaning clients start saving money the day they meet you—and you're getting a piece of the savings. They don't spend a single extra penny from their pocket. A win–win.

And clients are thrilled with your service because a) you come to them whenever they want and wherever they are, and b) you have great ideas that really help them. Now, rather than trying to hang on to clients who may make one or two purchases with you over a few years, you have scads of clients who use your rescue service once, and then use all of your financial offerings for the rest of their lives.

You take the time to break down your process and write a little one-page manual. You recruit other financial planners with great energy and passion and send them off to resuscitate more clients in their own vans. Before you know it, you've got a franchise.

Who knew that just being you would pay off so well? And now with all that extra income you are making, the trifocals are gone (thanks, LASIK surgery). But that no. 2 pencil? She's staying. Nothing will ever take the good old no. 2 from you. Not even tons of cash.

CHAPTER FIVE

HOW WE DO THINGS DOWN ON THE FARM

I've probably forced you to face some hard truths so far, and you may be feeling a little nervous. But buck up! Now it's time to work this plan.

From here on out we're taking our cues from Chuck Radcliffe and the other giant-pumpkin growers who follow the kill/nurture process and turn out prizewinner after prizewinner. This is the system I followed that helped me build my own multimillion-dollar companies. And if you do nothing else, this is the process that will help grow your business and get your life back. (Of course, you have to follow the *whole* Pumpkin Plan if you want to grow your business into the powerhouse you always dreamed it would be. But this is a really, *really* good start.)

Kill First, Nurture Later

Removing less-promising pumpkins from the vine is standard operating procedure for Chuck Radcliffe, Howard Dill and all other giant pumpkin farmers. There is no mercy here, no "Aw shucks, it may grow big one day." There is no "Geez, this sure is a pretty pumpkin; it makes my garden look more impressive." And they don't say, "Who cares if it stays there? It's going to rot away, anyway. It's not hurting anyone." They just kill it . . . fast.

Farmers know which pumpkins they need to pull off the vine based on which pumpkins are growing faster, which pumpkins have damage or blight and which pumpkins have the strongest root system. If you created an Assessment Chart in the previous chapter, you've already figured out which plants (clients) are the strongest and which are the weakest. Now, it's time for the kill.

You may be tempted to just jump right into the nurturing. You might be thinking, "I cannot afford to lose a single client, so I'll just focus on growing my relationships with my top clients. Plus, I saw *Children of the Corn*. The farmers are fucking crazy. They'll kill *anything*. Not me, Malachi. Not me."

Buzzzzzz! (That's the sound of my annoying game-show buzzer going off.) As long as you let these rotting pumpkins stay connected to your vine, you can't do the work needed to actually grow those good relationships because you're already too stretched as it is. And even if you aren't playing the entrepreneur's five-to-nine game, you can't devote yourself to everyone, all the time. It's just impossible. You need time and energy for a deep dive, and you can't do that if you don't kill first.

Last year my friend and colleague Sarah Shaw (I consider her my sister. We are *that* close. We share *that many* Immutable Laws.)

mentioned that her brother John had read *The Toilet Paper Entrepreneur* in his off season (shock of shocks, I instantly liked the guy) and started implementing a couple of the key strategies, to great success. "Off season?" I asked. "What does your brother do?"

"He installs solar panels. His revenue has doubled in the last year," Sarah said. Doubled? I had to call this guy.

So I called up John Shaw of Colorado-based Shaw Solar (genius name, John) and got the lowdown on his business.

Shaw Solar is now the top provider of solar panels for homes and small commercial buildings such as restaurants and gyms. Being number one in any industry or region is impressive, of course, but John's accomplishment is truly a major feat. "I live in a town of about 18,000 people, in a county of about 45,000. It's a small market, and we have thirty solar contractors here. There are literally five pages of solar contractors in the phone book. Of the thirty, four of us are making a living installing solar, and two of us are making a fantastic living doing it."

Sounds like two great pumpkins to me. And a remaining field of unremarkables.

Solar is a growth industry, and John is doing better than the national average in a totally saturated (and some might say, tapped out) market. So how did John grow his very own giant (solar) pumpkin? Simple. He killed off the clients who weren't cutting it and then came up with ingenious ways to service those who were.

"I realized I was spreading myself too thin in certain areas," John explained. "I remember you said you can be great at one thing, maybe two, if you're lucky, and that you should exploit the hell out of those things and outsource the rest. The second point that really hit home was, don't be afraid to say no to the stuff you're not great at or isn't a good fit, because the moment you say no, you become a hot commodity." It's true. Just think back to the last time you were a free agent—you never had any problem getting a date when you already had someone steady, right? It kind of works like that.

John had been ready for a while to make a change. He was completely at capacity. "I couldn't work one minute more. I left the house at 4:30 a.m. and rolled in after 7:00 p.m. My wife and daughter were becoming strangers to me. I was maxed out and I wondered, how could I work less and still grow my business? Reading your book gave me the confidence to make the tough decisions I'd been afraid to make." (At this point I was totally in love with John.)

So here's what I learned about installing solar energy equipment. According to John, installing solar electric panels is a pretty simple process. John doesn't have to spend a lot of time on the job site overseeing staff, and it all gets done pretty quickly. Installing solar hot-water heaters, on the other hand, is much more complicated. There are a ton of moving parts—which are more expensive than the parts required for installing solar electric panels. "Most people screw it up," John explained. "We don't, but I do have to be on the job site pretty much the whole time. So it costs more in terms of costs of goods, and time."

Even though John knew installing solar hot water systems was taking up fifty percent of his time while earning him ten percent of his revenue, and even though he knew that he made at least twice as much per hour installing solar electric, he still couldn't let solar hot water go. He had marketed Shaw Solar as a full-service solar contractor, and he was worried that if he said no to solar water, word would get out and he would lose solar electric jobs to contractors who claimed to handle both. "But then I thought, 'full-service contractor' is my thing only because I wrote it down. Why do I have to do it? I decided to say no to all but the best, most high-profile solar hot water jobs." John took the "say no" lesson to heart and almost overnight, he became a hot commodity.

Key distinction here: John started "killing off" solar hot water customers by limiting the *service* he provided. It's not that he was telling existing clients to take a hike—John's customers are usually one-offs and aren't likely to need solar services again in the near future.

As soon as John killed off nearly all of the solar hot water clients, something very interesting happened. He didn't just have more time to focus on the more profitable, less complicated solar electric projects. He *tripled* his solar electric work.

Huh? How did that happen?

As John mentioned, in my first book I talked about how saying no to someone makes you a hot commodity. When a prospect called John and asked him to hook them up with solar hot water, he told them no. At least half the time the prospect would ask, "Well, what *can* I buy from you?" They just wanted solar—solar *anything*.

"Before I started saying no, I would have installed a solar water system on a customer's house for ten grand, and because it was labor intensive and required my supervision, made very little money. Now, we have a twenty-minute conversation, I say no, and I'm installing a solar electric system on a customer's house for forty grand. I'm not selling snake oil, or even upselling, I'm really not. It's just different things. Do you want a car, or a motorcycle? Solar hot water and solar electric both make energy, they both have value, but they're different."

Now, John doesn't have to be on the job site as much. He spends more time at home with his family, and when he is home, he's more present for them. He has more time and energy to actually develop his business, and takes the necessary time to build the processes for installing solar electric perfectly every single time. He is no longer running around in reactionary mode, getting dirty every day on a roof or in a mechanical room, frantically trying to get it all done. (Remember the hamster on the wheel? Yeah. That was him.)

In just one year, a year in which John and his crew took off of work for *three months*, which they had not done the year before, Shaw Solar doubled its revenue. Despite the shorter season, they went from $800,000 to $1.6 million in revenue. Take an extra three months off, double the revenue! Suck it, workaholics. Suck it.

That is something worth killing for.

When addressing any problem in your business, or any opportunity, you have to ask "who?" first, not "how?" If you start by asking, "How do I do this?" the burden becomes yours. You'll have to spend more time figuring it out, you'll feel more overwhelmed and in the end, you still won't be dealing with the core problem. Move one stinking letter and you've got the answer you need. Simply by moving the "w," your job becomes making the system that can support the "who," and then making it repeatable. The who question keeps you focused on your top clients.

The solution that finally got John unstuck and off the hamster wheel was all about the "who." When he stopped trying to figure out how to work less and grow his business and focused on whom he wanted to provide services for—people who wanted solar electric—it became easy to say no to those he did *not* want to provide services for—people who wanted solar hot water—and everything clicked. The "work less" part and "grow the business" part happened naturally. And in the end, he got way more than he bargained for.

"I'm not really motivated by money," John had explained when we started our little chat. "We were doing fine financially before I changed course, but now I have the resources to *really* grow my business." See? He's thinking about that next seed.

KILLING 101

Now it's time to remove the weeds, the diseased pumpkins and any other distractions so that your existing top clients, and other new clients just like them, can start blossoming. If this step totally freaks you out, go back to your Assessment Chart and find the client who is the biggest pain in the ass and who, when fired, will have the least financial impact on your business. Fire them first. See how relieved you are when the pain in the ass isn't calling you anymore? With your most cringe-worthy client out of the way, notice how you have more time to focus on your other clients.

If you're still feeling nervous, remember, if you fire that first client and the world collapses—it won't—you can always go back to the jerk. They'll give you the old "I told you so," take you back, and treat you like garbage, like they did before. So know this, if I am wrong (which I'm not), you can easily get diseased clients back (which you shouldn't) . . . if you really want to (which you won't).

It's common for entrepreneurs to reverse this part of the plan, which is a mistake. They think firing clients is too risky, because they're afraid the better clients will never come. So they reverse the plan, opting to try and get better clients *first* and then get rid of the crap clients.

Reversing the plan doesn't work because it takes time to cultivate relationships with your top clients and attract new, better clients. And no matter how many appointments you move around and how many energy drinks you guzzle, you do not have the time. The Pumpkin Plan is not an "if you build it, they will come" kind of plan. This is a "build it, then build a paved road to your client's door, then give them a luxury bus ride (while serving them breakfast using only the finest china) to your door" kind of plan, and you need all of the extra time and emotional energy you can get to pull it off.

I get that you're nervous, so stage the process for your own comfort. It's a lot of work to weed the entire patch in one shot. And, because you can't perfectly evaluate new clients coming on board, you will get some bummers—weeds keep coming back, whether you like it or not. So think of your killing as more calculated than a spree.

So how do you fire a client? Here are four ways to go about it, without straight-up telling them . . . or actually killing them. (Last time I checked, that was pretty much outlawed in all fifty states . . . Jersey is questionable.)

1. *Eliminate services.* This was John Shaw's strategy, and you saw how well that worked for him. If you're truly trying to get rid of a specific client, or a group of clients, because they're just downright nasty, just telling them you no longer offer one service so they don't come back and ask for your other services may not work; you may have to go about it differently. For example, you might eliminate a specific service, or you might eliminate servicing a specific type of company (the same type of company your sucky client has . . . what a coincidence). To do this, use the industry expertise trick. Explain that "We have shifted all of our resources to serve an industry other than yours, and we can no longer help you."

2. *Prioritize the stars.* Simply prioritize your best clients. When the good ones call, they get serviced first. The cringe-worthy

clients get pushed to the back of the line. When you're on the phone with a cringemeister and a star client calls, you (politely) hang up on the cringe client and move on to the good guy. The cringers will get the hint. Sure, it's a little bit *Mean Girls*, but it gets the job done.

3. *Raise prices.* If you really want to see bad clients run for the hills, raise your prices. And I don't mean a measly 10 or 20 percent. Increase your fees until it becomes prohibitive for the client. In rare cases, some clients will just rise to the occasion, paying you seriously good money just to keep working with you. And because these people probably want to work with you, they'll probably be nicer, too. This is because dollars act like appreciation points—if you raise your prices, your perceived value goes up, and suddenly you're not their personal whipping boy. Because they are paying you real coin, they're motivated for you to succeed. They can't afford you failing. So they become all nicey-nice and help you. Sweet!

4. *Refuse to two-time.* Another way of breaking ties with a diseased client is to explain to them that you have an agreement with a major client that prohibits you from servicing them any longer. Now, I am not suggesting you create a contract or any of that; the goal here is to have an explanation for the break. This is like the world of dating—you explain to the cringer that you are going steady with someone else. Just give your major client a heads-up—and get their nod of approval—that you are going to pin your breakup with a bad client on serving them (your good guy) better.

A small note about change: Though occasionally your annoying, disrespectful, demanding clients will pull a 180 in response to your attempt to kill them off, it is very rare. Most sucky people don't suddenly become unsucky, or even tolerable. Don't expect it—and certainly don't expect it from the rat bastards who make you cringe when you hear their voice or see their face. Don't use this kill strategy as a wake-up call for abusive clients—they will never wake up. Just kill the blight, and move on.

The killing is not over yet. It is not just the asshole clients that have to go; it's the ones who aren't a good fit, too. You may have the nicest people in the world buying from you. The Dalai Lama may be knocking at your door, begging to buy shoes from you. But if you make hats (and not shoes), you still need to kill off the relationship. Even great, friendly, nice customers need to go away *if* they are unfit for your offering. But because these folks are nice, they will thank you when you kill them off—if you do it right.

When the nice folks (which, by the way, probably describes 95 percent or more of your clients) want to do business with you, but are unfit, you "kill" the relationship by introducing them to another vendor who can serve them perfectly (more on this later). At the end of the day, they want great service. And you are giving them great service by introducing them to someone else who can serve them best. See, killing is for nice people, too.

One thing to remember is that, just as in a pumpkin patch, weeding is a constant process. Companies change and clients come and go. Once you get the hang of filling it out, make time to create a new Assessment Chart every quarter. Block off a day or two to evaluate customers and make the tough decisions that you are, by now, accustomed to making. You never know when a pesky little weed or diseased pumpkin might worm its way in and take over your entire patch.

Work the Plan—
Take Action in 30 Minutes (or Less)

I. *Make a "Most (Not) Wanted" list.* Looking at your Assessment Chart, make a list of clients who just have to go.

2. *Determine your kill strategy.* Whether you decide to raise your prices, eliminate services, de-prioritize, contractually block or just tell them flat out, you need a plan. Determine which strategy would be most effective, taking into account the client's influence in your industry.

3. *Fire that first rotten client.* Go for it. Now is the time. Send the email. Make the call. Or, if you still have both of your nuts, do it face to face. Things are about to get a whole lot better.

How to Pumpkin Plan Your Industry — Personal Services

Imagine you operate a dog-walking and dog-sitting business. Hang up the leashes, step over the slobbery chew toys and shut the little rascals out of your office while we Pumpkin Plan this business.

You operate one of five dog-walking/sitting businesses in your area, and competition is stiff. Every time you hang up a flyer, one of your competitors hangs one up over yours. Because you're competing on price, the only way you can make any serious money is if you walk eight to ten dogs at one time. And even when you can get that many dogs at one time, you're still struggling to get by.

After you figure out who your top clients are, you call them up and ask to meet with them. You learn that many of them are frustrated with the fact that their dog is just one of dozens of dogs you take care of at the same time, and they wish their dog received more of your attention. Some of them want to know more about how their dogs are doing and to feel connected to their dogs, even though they can't be with them. (Loads of guilt here, people. Loads of guilt.)

You decide to let a few of your most challenging clients go, the ones who constantly "forget" to pay you. It pains you a bit to see your competitors snap them up—they already have so many dogs. But, they are the ones who will now have to deal with the "forgotten" payments.

And that's when it hits you—you could do the opposite of what your competitors do. Rather than walk many dogs at one time, you could offer an exclusive dog-walking service. You could offer the highest-end dog-walking service in the world. You could take little Bruno out for a hike all by himself, and charge double . . . triple . . . four times what the competition charges. And, of course, you wouldn't be labeled as a "dog walker" any more. Businesses with those kinds of labels don't make much. But a "canine caregiver"—heck, that's what you are now . . . and *that* label gets paid beaucoup bucks. Listening to your clients' Wish List, it is clear that that's what they want—someone who will take care of the physical *and* emotional health of their dogs.

Now, you *only* offer one-on-one dog-care services. You take dogs for long hikes. You set up playdates with their doggie friends. You text their "mommy" and "daddy" photos of their adventures. You groom the dogs, keeping their fur clean and their nails cut.

You teach the dogs new commands and improve their doggie play-ground manners, so much so that their owners can walk through the park again without wearing a disguise. You leave thoughtful notes describing everything you and their "baby" did that day. And when you dog-sit overnight, you spend most of your time there, rather than just come over in time to let them out at night. It's just you and the dog, chilling out watching Lifetime movies and eating ice cream.

The comments pour in from customers about how amazed they are by their "new and improved" pets. Better manners, better behavior, better everything. You are giving people the dog they always dreamed about! Wow!

Because you charge a premium for this service, you can hire other people to be canine caregivers for you. And because you have this whole thing down, you can easily train them to coddle those little pooches just as you would—as *your clients* would, if they were there.

Now, you have the hottest, busiest, most profitable canine-caregiver business in the state. People tell you that you should write a book about it . . . come out with your own line of doggie supplies and baked goods . . . open up a doggie B&B. "Maybe," you think. "We'll see." You can do whatever you want. You're the biggest pumpkin around.

CHAPTER SIX

THE TOURNIQUET TECHNIQUE

Luke's web-programming company brings in $500,000 a year. He is thirty years old, talented, going places. He is also broke. He borrows money from his wife, who does her best to support him, and he just took out a $20,000 loan from his parents to cover . . . oh, this one hurts . . . *payroll*. Ouch, right? It's not even an expansion loan. It's a freakin' Band-Aid . . . over a gigantic, gaping, oozing hole.

When we sat down to brainstorm how to stop the bleeding and get him back onto solid ground, what do you think he said? Just guess. It's a common refrain, one I've already talked about, one you've probably said to yourself or someone else, probably more than once. (Hint: Remember wedding florist Bruce, driving around in his Escalade, leveraged to the hilt?)

"We're just one project away. Once these people sign, we'll be good."

Uh-huh.

I wanted to tell him his latest Hail Mary pass client wasn't going to cure the disease that's eating away at his company, his bank account, his dreams. Instead, I thought *I'm just going to pretend you didn't just say that and try to fix this, for real.*

Let me fill you in on Luke. He's been one project away from making it for eight years. *Eight years.* He doesn't pay himself much—a full-time job at Mickey D's would net more cash—but he does pay eight employees, with a little help from his wife and his parents. Luke is in so deep, there are only two ways out: cut expenses or close up shop. So I give it to him straight: "You have to fire someone."

I could see by the look on Luke's face (have you seen *Scream*?) that he wasn't buying it. He was horrified. I wasn't surprised. No one ever wants to fire someone. Entrepreneurs *really* don't want to fire their employees. We think our team is special. Bound for greatness. A family unit dedicated to helping us make real the dreams that were once just doodles on cocktail napkins. Our egos won't let us fire anyone. Where would Melissa find another job like this one? How would Derek cope? What if Nikki can't afford COBRA?

I get it. I do. I've had to let truly amazing people go during lean times, and it has dropped me to my knees in a sobbing mess. No question, it sucks. But you know what sucks more? Letting *everyone* go, including yourself, because of bankruptcy. And that's exactly where Luke was headed if he didn't face facts and trim his staff.

"But if this new client signs, I'll need all of my people," Luke protests.

"No, Luke. We have to find a way to service these clients with you and three employees."

Now Luke is really upset. I can almost hear his inner freak-out: *Fire* five *employees! No way! I can't do that. Who would I fire? How would I choose? What if we can't handle the workload? I can't work any harder than I already am.*

I met Luke while doing a presentation at Harvard and we've been friends ever since. I care for Luke like a brother. I do. And I know exactly how he feels. I know what it's like to push yourself every day so you can pay people who make more than you do. I know what it feels like to wake up the morning after you miraculously cover payroll and realize it's starting all over again, and in two weeks you'll have to pull yet another twenty, thirty, forty thousand out of your ass. And I know that no matter how much good sense it makes, firing more than half of your staff just feels like you've failed. So I'm gentle when I show him exactly why he *must* do it.

"Luke, you can't afford eight employees with $500,000 in annual revenue. No one can. It doesn't mean you've screwed up. The numbers wouldn't add up for anybody," I assured him. "You've been at this almost ten years, and if you don't make a change now, you're going to end up letting *everyone* go in the very near future . . . because you're going to have to close your doors for good."

Luke was quiet, so I knew he was ready to at least consider my advice. I took a look at his client roster. From the outside it looked like his web-programming business was tightly focused. All of his clients had a similar function, and required a similar end result. It seemed easy to systematize. He shouldn't need so many people servicing clients. So what was up with that?

"Why do you need so many people?" I asked.

"Well, some of the coding is in C++, some in PHP, some in Ruby, some in flash; some is in all different languages. I need people who know how to handle the various coding requirements." In other words, some of their work was in Japanese, some was in English and some was a combination of pig latin, sign language and Klingon.

Bingo! That's his problem. He was loaded up with coding linguists so that he could take on projects in every possible language, and he needed staff to handle all of these oddball requests. No wonder he was going broke. Luke may have had one type of service, but he wasn't really serving a niche client base—he was saying yes to everyone, still playing the quantity game, still trying to land any and all clients, even if it meant he was overstaffed and overextended. He was holding out hope that the demand for all of the languages his company provided coding in would increase, and suddenly having eight people on payroll would make perfect sense. Luke was running around the pumpkin patch that was his business, trying to water and fertilize and love every single bloom on the vine.

But that's not how you grow a giant pumpkin, is it?

"Luke, if you only work on projects coded in one language—the one that brings in the most revenue and is the easiest to service—you can handle it with three employees," I said, expecting to see a giant light bulb go on over his head, expecting him to high-five me and do a little dance . . . okay, maybe that's pushing it, but I had just figured out how to save his ass. I'm not saying he had to break-dance or anything, but a little end-zone happy dance would have been appreciated.

"But Mike, most of my clients will tell me to F off!"

"Perfect! You don't want to service them anyway. You want to work with your top clients and expand your business from there. It's the nature of the beast. You're going to piss off a few people who aren't your top clients."

"Mike, I just can't. It's too big of a risk. I *need* all of my clients."

Sigh.

Luke is one of those people who, like most of us, couldn't shift his mentality, even if it meant saving his business. He wanted to get off the hamster wheel, but he was scared to jump, so he ended up running and running to nowhere. And he'll keep running . . . until he collapses (or his business does). I fear that bankruptcy is going to be one of Luke's lessons, and it's not necessary.

No matter how much you think they need you, no matter how much *you* think you need *them*, you can't keep employees you can't afford. Period. The beauty of the Pumpkin Plan is that once you kill off the diseased and unfit clients and shift your attention to your most promising clients, you have the opportunity to cut all expenses that don't serve your top clients—everything from phone lines to parking spaces. It makes cutting expenses so much easier. You can see what has to go, and because you're trying to grow a massive, prize-winning pumpkin, you have the emotional leverage to get real with your P&L and stop the bleeding. I call it the "Tourniquet Technique."

Stop the bleeding

I've said this before, many, *many* times, but it's worth saying several million times more: cash is the lifeblood of your business. It's more important than your massive inventory, unpaid receivables and impressive lines of credit. Inventory can end up in a landfill, customers may never pony up and lines of credit vanish in the blink of an eye. Like Luke, you'll never make it if you don't have enough cash—and I'm willing to bet you don't have enough of it.

Most entrepreneurs are broke, strapped, or on their way to the red. Why? Because of human nature. We spend what we earn, whether it's five thousand, fifty thousand or five *hundred* thousand. You finally land that huge client and suddenly you need a new assistant, or new office space, or a new corner booth at the next trade show. Your product suddenly becomes the hottest thing ever and you're expanding into new areas that have little to do with your original concept. When you should be shoring up reserves for rainy days (and hurricanes) or to get you over the hump during that tricky "growth period," you're signing checks like Trump, without a care in the world.

Until you run out of cash.

And you will run out of cash . . . unless you stop the bleeding.

The Pumpkin Plan isn't just about revenue; it's about profit. Remember profit? That's why you got into this crazy business in the first place—to turn a profit. A huge, mother of a profit that will make your life . . . am I right? If turning a profit is not high on your priority list, you're reading the wrong book. May I suggest you read the *Watermelon Wash-up, Calamity Cantaloupe*, or the *Failure Fruit Cup*?

Simply put, the Tourniquet Technique is a method for reducing or eliminating expenses associated with the clients who ranked the lowest on your Client Assessment Chart, those Grade F, diseased pumpkins you got rid of right off the bat. They're not just annoying and time consuming, they're bloodsuckers. You have a whole host of expenses related to keeping your worst clients happy. So, before you bleed out, apply the tourniquet. Look at your expenses—everything from employees to office supplies—and cut anything related specifically to your most cancerous clients.

It seems elementary. *Like, duh! Why wouldn't I cut expenses related to a client after I fire them, Mike?*

Because you're human, that's why. You're going to keep spending what you earn and feed yourself and your company a line
about why it's probably a good idea to *keep* spending. You don't
want to fire Nicole in accounting just because although she used
to spend 85 percent of her day chasing down your bastard clients,
she now has nothing to do. So what if she's filed and re-filed in-
voices seventeen times this week? Nicole's awesome. And she has
three kids. Three adorable, helpless, expensive kids. You'll find
something for her to do.

That showroom space you rented to impress that client (aka
public enemy number one)? You're not going to give that up. It's
cool. It makes you feel important when you drive by and see
your company name on the door. So what if it's eating up 10 percent of your budget? It's a great space. You'll find *something* to do
with it.

And don't even get me started on the national conference. You
have to go. Sure, you started attending because those needy clients
expected you to show up every year and show them a good time.
But it's probably good for business. Now that you're "single" at the
conference, moving freely without your ball-and-chain client,
you'll probably land some *new* clients. (Ahem . . . maybe clients
just like the ones you ditched.) Besides, everyone is really excited
about going this year. It's a real bonding experience for your staff.
You'll find *something* worthwhile at the event.

It's hard to say goodbye to clients, even the jerkwads. It's also
hard to say goodbye to the world you built up around them—the
people, stuff and services you paid for just to keep the jerkwads
happy. As much as you love Nicole, that hip showroom space and
getting away for a work-cation every year, you have to stop the
bleeding—you have to love your business *more*.

QUESTION EVERYTHING, LINE BY LINE

It was supposed to be a side business, a fun project that might possibly net them a few extra bucks. When Athelia Wolley and her former business partner launched ShabbyApple.com, they hoped to sell twenty, maybe thirty different styles of dresses a year, nothing huge. They loved the clothing women wore in the forties and fifties and realized that behind the *Mad Men* trend and Martha Stewart's domesticity empire was a yearning for a time gone by. Athelia noticed that women who shared her Immutable Laws romanticized the past, and therefore the dresses.

Having worked for Amnesty International, Athelia was committed to manufacturing the dresses according to human-rights standards (that is, no five-year-olds pulling twelve-hour days in sweatshops), which meant the dresses would cost more to make. To keep prices down, the cofounders decided to forgo the margins of wholesale and sell directly to consumers via ShabbyApple.com. But this meant they had to figure out how to get the word out about the line on their own, without the help of a retailer.

Like most start-ups, Shabby Apple had almost no money for marketing or advertising. To build brand recognition, other designers hire fashion publicists, pay to have their line in a show-room and hire a team to help them create lookbooks (a kind of mini-catalog or brochure for magazines and retailers) and other marketing materials. But unless you're a design savant, or already famous, or the luckiest person on earth, this process can take years and cost a fortune.

Necessity is the badass mother of invention, so you know this story is heading for a happy ending. I mean, how many great success stories start out with, "We had no money, so . . ." Tons. Shabby Apple is one of those success stories. Today they sell more than one hundred different designs through their website. Athelia left her job and now operates ShabbyApple.com full time . . . and she's kicking butt.

I had to figure out how she and her former business partner were able to rise to the top in the saturated, cutthroat fashion industry—and with a product that cost more to make. (Don't you want to know, too?) So I called her up and grilled her for about an hour, and being the lovely woman she is, Athelia indulged me.

"We chose to market online rather than sell to wholesalers because most people shop online, especially women," she explained. "The second reason is, it allows us to have lower prices, and if we were selling through a wholesaler it would cut our margins a lot, and with our higher manufacturing costs, we would not be able to pull it off."

But how did she build a customer base with no marketing budget? Athelia's light-bulb moment came when she noticed that her friends—women in their thirties with small children—read blogs every day, looking for cooking tips, vacation ideas and fashion trends. So she started sending samples to bloggers who, in turn, talked up Shabby Apple on their blogs. In the beginning they split their marketing budget on bloggers and advertising, but soon discovered that they got *way* more sales from a mention on a blog post than they did from expensive, targeted advertising.

"There weren't a lot of companies focused on the blogging market—I still don't think companies have capitalized on that market," she said. They used the (free!) tracking software, Google Analytics, to figure out exactly who their top customers were. "Google will tell you how many hits you get from certain blogs.

Or we would give a blog a certain coupon code. You can track where your sales are coming from. That was really helpful."

Because Athelia's top clients were women in their thirties who shop online and read blogs, she was able to save Shabby Apple a boatload of money—around $20,000 a month she might have been spending for showroom, publicist and other fees most fashion designers count as necessary expenses. Despite their massive growth, they still only spend around $1,000 each month marketing via blogs. Amazing, right?

If Athelia had set out to market Shabby Apple to all women, or had decided their clothing had to be sold retail, would they be a giant pumpkin right now? Maybe. Or maybe Athelia would still be working her full-time job, trying to make a go of her "side" business on evenings or weekends.

Do you see how focusing on her ideal (top) customers allowed Athelia to eliminate expenses that most designers must incur? Most people in her industry would have told her she was crazy not to hire a publicist to pitch her collection to magazines, that she absolutely *had* to have a showroom in New York, that advertising was just part of the equation. Wrong! She's saving close to a quarter-million dollars every year, just by thinking about what her customers want, how to reach them, and then doing just that— and *only* that.

Now that you know who your top clients are, take a good, hard, open-minded look at your expenses. Is everything *really* necessary? Could you change the way you market to your clients to better serve them? Do you really need to throw the annual party if your top clients really don't do parties? If it turns out that your top clients conduct business primarily online, do you really need a glossy brochure?

Go through everything, line by line, and ask yourself, "Does this serve my best clients best?" If it doesn't, let it go.

THE RIGHT WAY TO STAFF A GIANT PUMPKIN

Maybe you haven't created an organizational chart for your business yet, but I'm willing to bet that, if you have, you've approached it the same way most entrepreneurs do—working with what *is*, instead of what *should be*. I'm willing to bet I'm right, because just about everyone does this.

It seems logical to make a diagram listing you and all of your employees and their job descriptions, and then try to figure out how to make *that* work. ('Cause I know you *really, really* want to make it work.) But you don't just want to figure out how to make your current setup work; you want to figure out how to grow a multimillion-dollar business that dwarfs the competition, freeing you from spinning your wheels . . . forever. So while it may seem logical to start with what you've got, the right way to staff your giant pumpkin is to start with what you wish you had.

Your main objective is to serve the hell out of your top clients, so your org chart (let's just abbreviate, shall we?) should support that. So first, you need to create the ideal org chart, one that, if actualized, would enable you to support your top clients efficiently and with ease. No stress. No freak-outs. No missed deadlines. What would that look like? Would you eliminate certain positions? Would you create a new role? Would you set up teams to share the load?

At this stage, your organization is not about your personnel; it's about the positions. Stop thinking about the people who work for you and what they do. Think instead about the roles and responsibilities of the positions that best serve your top clients. How would the people in those positions communicate with each other? How would they report to each other?

Now that you have an ideal org chart, plug your staff into the roles they should be filling. Often, some people (yourself included) will be wearing many hats. You may have an org chart with fifty positions to be filled by ten people. And sometimes, there will be people currently working for your firm who don't fit in the ideal org chart. Just because you have fifty positions for ten people, doesn't mean everyone will fit in. It's backwards to draw an org chart based on the current structure of a struggling business because the org chart is partly to blame for the struggle in the first place. The key is to draw the ideal chart, and then plug in the pieces of your existing business that fit properly.

Before I did this exercise with Luke, he was absolutely positive he couldn't fire *anyone* or he wouldn't have enough people to handle the workload. He couldn't see how to make it work, and you probably can't either.

Now you and I know that Luke needs to tighten his focus and get rid of all of those coding variations, but even if he doesn't follow my advice, he can make a few staffing adjustments that will dramatically change his bottom line—for the better.

When we compared his ideal org chart with his actual org chart, I noticed that Luke had three project managers (PMs), one of whom was basically unbillable and a distraction to the company. However, his office manager (OM) was extraordinary, and had the time and skills to take on some of the project management. So I showed Luke that if he fired his dead-weight PM, his OM could handle it, no problem.

You know what else we noticed? Luke was handling five or six responsibilities that he shouldn't have been handling at all. He was spending just 10 percent of his time in his CEO role because he was busy doing the jack-of-all-trades thing entrepreneurs do so well . . . or rather, so often. (It's a disease, I swear.) He was marketing, he was selling, he was handling HR issues, he was doing the bookkeeping and, in his spare time (of which there wasn't any), he was actually coding. That's right. He was doing the work he pays eight employees to do. It was all right there, in color-coded glory. The org chart doesn't lie.

I know how scary it is even contemplating this level of change, but you've got to do it. Awareness is everything, and one of the best ways you can get real about your staff is to create these org charts—visual representations of your ideal chart and your actual chart. When you can see how it should be and also how it is, you can then shift people and responsibilities around until you can't tell the two charts apart.

And *that*, my friend, is how you staff a giant pumpkin.

Work the Plan—
Take Action in 30 Minutes (or Less)

I. *Start with the easy and obvious.* Now that you've fired your most rotten clients, cut all expenses related to those clients, or those types of clients. For example, maybe you can get rid of that pricey software, or the part-time administrative staffer you dedicated to serving this now-fired client's every whim.

2. *Cut to serve.* Now review all of your expenses and determine a) if they help you serve your top clients the way they really want to be served, and b) how you could modify or cut these expenses to *better* serve your top clients.

3. *Chart it.* Create the ideal org chart. Now, start plugging the right people into the right spots so they can serve the right customers in the right way. Execute on this, and yours will be the fattest pumpkin in town.

How to Pumpkin Plan Your Industry — Artists

Let's pretend you're in a rock band—playing sort of a throwback to old-school punk rock—with breakout potential. Set your guitar down, pull up your skinny jeans, and let's get to work Pumpkin Planning this business—because unless you're just playing the art-for-art's-sake game, or just hanging out in your garage, this *is* a business.

You're band is about to "blow up," as they say. You're close to making it big . . . but you've been close for five years now (or has it been fifteen?—boy, does time fly), and you're really sick of temping at offices just to make ends meet. You're lucky because, unlike your major influences, you don't have to wait around for a record label to pick you up. Technology has advanced to the point where you can just create and distribute and market your own stuff. (Now do you see that you are a business?)

When you do the Assessment Chart, you choose your best fans as your clients—the people who buy everything you put out, show up at all of your gigs and talk about you to everyone they know, whenever they can. By definition, your raving fans are your top clients. But you have a few big "fans" that just don't get you. They come to your shows, but they sing along so loudly you can't hear yourself think, try to break into backstage and touch you when you walk through the crowd, and constantly hog your free stuff (you had to stop throwing T-shirts into the crowd, because these fans would hurt others to get them— not to wear them, but to sell them on eBay). Put them at the bottom of your chart.

Really, you just want to figure out what your biggest fans—your top clients—have on their Wish List. So you call them up, and after they stop shrieking and ugly crying, "Oh my gawd!", you ask them about their frustrations with their favorite bands (not just yours) and with the music industry in general. And you start to realize that the people who love you best really want to feel special. They don't like feeling like stupid fans, waiting outside for a photo or an autograph. They want the inside track—they want to be in on what goes on behind the scenes, the creative process.

But you can't make thousands of people feel special.

Or can you?

You and your bandmates put your punk-rock heads together and come up with a way to let fans into your lives in a controlled way that could be accessible to everyone. You decide to document the creation of your next album, your next gig, your next tour, on video and in photographs. You live-Tweet from your studio sessions. You put questions out to your fans via Facebook, asking for input on a song. You stop hosting generic meet and greets after shows and start hosting parties instead, where you just hang out with fans. You respond to fans' questions on your blog. Oh—and you do the coolest thing any band has ever done: you embed passwords in your songs. Codes in the lyrics that give your truest, biggest fans who are in the know, access to a treasure trove of exclusive material you have on a protected website.

Now, your top clients—your raving fans—*love you* even more than before, *and* they now have scads of content to pass around to all of their peeps. It is hard—scratch that, it is *impossible*—for them to keep the passwords secret. So they blurt them out to everyone they know, and everyone they know starts listening to your stuff because they want to be the next to discover the newest password.

Your top clients go absolutely nuts every time you mention their names or respond to them, and re-Tweet it to the whole freakin' world. Now you've got a new following of raving fans that want in on all of this, too. Your raving fans set up online communities, have their own meet-ups, write fan fiction about you. Soon, you're Internet famous, and then the record companies come a-callin'. It's up to you if you want to take the deal or not. You don't really need it. You're reaping all of the rewards (and most of the profits) now as a big-ass, rockin' pumpkin.

CHAPTER SEVEN

PLAY FAVORITES AND BREAK RULES

Now that you've ranked your customers, fired the diseased troublemakers, redirected your unfit customers, cut unnecessary expenses and put in a healthy root system (your new org chart), your next objective is to focus your energy on your core client group. Your goal—your *mission*—is to keep these folks so happy you obliterate the possibility that they would ever leave you for the competition.

To do that, you're going to have to go against conventional wisdom (and your mom's strict orders). You're going to have to play favorites and break a few other "playground" rules. And you're going to have to up your game, wowing customers with your super awesome nurturing skills. Dazzle them with innovation and superior service. Defy their imagination. Offer solutions to their problems and answers to their prayers.

Your clients don't know you're working the Pumpkin Plan, so your top clients won't know they're your top clients until they become the objects of your undying nurturance. How will they know they're on the VIP list if you don't tell them? Actually, strike that. Talk is cheap. You've got to *show* them. If you want your top clients to know how much you care about them, you've got to do something to let them know you value their business and want to see them succeed.

This, my friend, is the fun part.

In the next few chapters I'll give you my entire bag of tricks, the strategies I've used to grow my relationships with top clients, attract new top clients and grow my businesses, and my friends' businesses, into multimillion-dollar machines. For now, let's just start with the easy stuff.

Favoritism . . . it's a good thing

You probably have a few favorite clients, the people you're always glad to see walk through the door, the businesses you'll bend over backwards to help because—go figure—you actually like them and want to do a good job for them. And you probably don't want your other clients to know who your favorite clients are, or even that you play favorites at all. So you try to keep it on the down low. You try to make sure all of your clients get what they need and no one feels left out or left behind.

I get it. I do. You're a nice person. You feel guilty giving preferential treatment and you'd feel really, really bad if your other clients found out about all of the favors you dish out to your "pets." But I am here to set you free from the shamefully shameful shame! Playing favorites is nothing to feel guilty about. It's simply good business. And it is mandatory for your success. But, you say, you're a nice person. Of course, but isn't it super nice to take care of people who take care of you? Remember, these nice clients pay you.

Playing favorites may be frowned upon on playgrounds, in families and in umpiring baseball games, but it's a winning strategy for businesses because your top clients *are* your favorite clients, and they need special treatment. How else are they going to *feel* special? Just be sure to check yourself and make sure you aren't playing favorites with clients who don't deserve it, clients who don't meet your basic top-client requirements.

The problem is, even though you've whittled down your client list so that only the top clients remain, not everyone can be a favorite. If you favor everyone, then you really don't have a favorite, do you? Shoot, you can't even have half of your clients be favorites. This is reserved for the select few, baby.

I have a good friend, Tommy Muenich. Okay, his name really isn't Tommy Muenich. Not even close. But he really is my good friend. I know I said I would name names for the real stories, but Tommy hit it big—real big. And a problem that some people run into when they hit it big is that everyone hits them up for money. So Tommy generously allowed me to share his story with you, under the condition that I disguise his identity. I'm not sure if "Tommy Muenich" is the name he had in mind—maybe something that makes him sound dangerous, like Bruce Bond, or a super sexy, easy to pronounce name like Mike Michalowicz. Sorry, Tommy.

So Tommy and I are in a mastermind group together, and in one of our meetings he told me about how he grew his company, and sold it for a cool $30 million. He did it in part by playing favorites with just a few of his 200 clients. How many is a few? In his case, nine.

"I decided I would focus on my top ten clients, because ten is an obvious number," Tommy explained to me when I asked him about his strategy. "But as I went through the list with my team, I realized I had to remove one of the clients from my 'top clients' list—Wal-Mart. They weren't good communicators, they only had expectations and they wouldn't give us any flexibility. So that's how my top ten list became my top nine list." Even though they had bought millions from him over the years, Wal-Mart didn't make the cut.

After he decided on his top nine clients, Tommy made them his priority in all facets of his business. He posted the list throughout the building and above everyone's desk and instructed his staff to attend to their needs first. If one of his top nine called when he was on the phone with a lower-ranking client, he would say, "I have an emergency; I'll have to call you back" and hang up so he could take the call. He listened to their ideas and concerns and modified products to give the top nine what they wanted—different packaging, a new price point, whatever he could do.

The rest of his clients simply weren't his number one priority. Even Wal-Mart. That isn't to say he didn't provide them and all his other clients with darn good service, but when a top-nine client demanded attention, they got *all* the attention. But even the other 191 clients benefited from the trickle-down effect—some of the special treatment rubbed off on them. Tommy and his staff became more efficient at making stuff and solving problems. When he fixed something for a top-nine client, he would fix it across the board, and because his clients all were in similar industries, it often benefited all of them.

When he sold his company, the good folks who bought it came up with a new, "smarter" rule: "Treat everyone as if he or she is the best client." Tommy stayed on for a bit to help with the transition, and the day the new owners came in, they took down his top nine list and said, "Everyone is number one."

Tommy vehemently advised them not to do it. He explained to them that you can't make everyone number one. He explained how his business actually thrived by focusing on the top nine. But they didn't listen.

In farming terms, making everyone a number-one client is like saying "Make every pumpkin a giant pumpkin." It never works. So how do you think that little strategy worked out for my friend's newly sold company? Badly. Very, very badly. In less than two years, they went out of business. They lost the $30 million they invested, plus another $5 million they spent running the business, by breaking the Pumpkin Plan rule: only treat the best customers the best. It's really that simple.

Like the obsessed pumpkin farmers who play music for their prizewinning contenders and protect the gigantic gourd with homemade fences flanked by guard dogs, you have to nurture the hell out of your top clients. These guys aren't running around trying to make sure all of the other pumpkins in their patch get the same perks. They're single-minded in their approach, showering their enormous pumpkins with everything they could possibly need in order to grow one big enough to break the world record.

Now I'm not saying you should ignore all of your other clients or treat them poorly. As a general rule, don't skimp on quality of product or service. It's bad for business. But do develop a different approach for your top clients. Push them to the front of the line. Drop everything for them. Interrupt meetings to deal with their crises. Dream up new and better ways to serve them. Anticipate their needs. Give them first dibs on new products or services. Accommodate their special requests. And most importantly, go out of your way to help them grow their own business. Build systems that cater to their needs. Not so coincidentally, other prospects who have similar needs will flock to you. Pretty cool.

The other "average" clients will benefit from the runoff. The improvements you make for the best clients will inevitably help the other guys, too. And who knows, one of those average guys may hit a growth spurt, or suddenly get with the program in other ways. When that happens, you've just landed a new top client.

One important rule I *don't* want you to break when it comes to clients is this: Never tell them they are VIPs. You want your top clients to think the way you treat them is simply your company's standard. If they think you only do awesome stuff for them because you told them they're your BFF, then they might assume you *can't* do it for someone else. Worse, they might start to take advantage of you. The cool thing about keeping your VIPs in the dark about their status is, if a VIP believes the way you handle them is how you handle all of your clients, you are more likely to develop systems to make sure that's true.

THE CUSTOMER *ISN'T* ALWAYS RIGHT

One of the biggest fallacies in business is that old adage, "The customer is always right." Stop for a minute and think about what that would actually *mean* for *you* if it were true. If "the customer" (translation: *everyone who wants to do business with you*) is always right, how can you possibly serve all of them well? Maybe you can keep some of them happy, but when you try to cater to all of your clients—top, bottom and everyone in between—you just end up being stretched too thin. You exhaust yourself trying to keep everyone happy, which is an impossible goal, anyway. You keep making mistakes and letting people down. Spinning plates, people. Spinning plates.

What's worse is, if you hold on to this "customer-is-always-right" attitude, inevitably you'll piss off one of your top clients, because you did something "right" for someone else and it distracted you, preventing you from doing something right for them. And we can't have that. So let's modify this old standard and make it true:

The customer is NOT always right, but . . .

The *right* customer IS always right.

If you defined your Immutable Laws and filled out your Assessment Chart, you should have a pretty good idea of who your top clients are, and what they have in common. These, your most promising clients, are the "right" clients, so they are allowed to be right . . . always. They can have (almost) anything they want, because they are your primary focus now. You want to discover all the right things you can do for them, since this will make you significantly better for them than your competition can dream of being.

Fortunately, your top clients are a lot alike. It's a safe bet that they all want something similar, that they will communicate with you in much the same way, that they will share similar expectations. And, because they share your Immutable Laws, they're probably a lot like you, too. It's a no-brainer. You've got this. You can absolutely adopt the "customer is always right" policy when you're only working with the right customers.

You're probably thinking, "What if my other, non-priority clients want to be right, too?" Well, first of all, *they do* want to be right. People will always want to be right and get what they want and feel important. But your focus is on the top clients—not just because you want them to be happy, not just because you want to cultivate and expand those relationships, but also because you want *more* clients just like them. You want their doppelgangers (but not the scary kind that show up in horror movies) so that you can grow your top-client list, adding other people and businesses who meet your requirements, clients who get what you're about and who have the potential to grow into a giant, record-breaking pumpkin.

Think of your business as a membership organization. All of the successful ones have rules on who can join. You need to be a graduate of *this* college, or you must participate *this* frequently, or you must pay *these* fees. They do everything they can to limit access or filter out the wrong members. You've got to have your own list of rules to help filter out clients—but keep it out of their sight line. The rules are for you and your team's eyes only.

Under-promise and Over-deliver

I live by this code, and you should, too. Everyone should. And because most people don't, adopting the Under-Promise, Over-Deliver (UPOD) rule gives you a serious advantage over, well, pretty much everyone.

Don't believe such a simple rule could have such a huge impact? Think of the last few times you had to meet with someone, and they told you when and where. I bet it went something like this:

"Meet me at the coffee shop at 2:30 p.m. today. Good?"

"Good! I'll see you then."

Two-thirty arrives, but they don't. There you sit in the coffee shop, waiting. Around 2:35, your phone rings. "I'm so sorry. I'm running late." (No kidding.) "I got stuck in traffic, my building was taken hostage by Justin Bieber fans and there is lava pouring out of the street . . . I'll be there in fifteen."

You're upset. Your colleague over-promised (2:30 p.m.) and then under-delivered (2:45 p.m.). But wait. It gets worse.

What happens when the clock strikes 2:45? Jack squat, that's what. Only this time, you don't even get a phone call.

Your colleague runs in around 2:55. He's sweating, but there's no Justin Bieber Fan Club shirt in sight, no lava-singed shoes. Your colleague just over-promised and under-delivered again, and you are pissed. I can guarantee you've had an under-deliver experience like this with someone recently and you were disappointed, upset or furious. It happens all the time.

Here's how that scenario could play out if your colleague practiced UPOD: You're scheduled to meet at 2:30 p.m. At nine in the morning you get a call that he is going to be late (he is habitually late), and will be there at 3:00. You're momentarily annoyed, but at least he gave you a heads-up, and you can schedule some extra work to get done before you head over to the coffee shop.

But here's the thing: your colleague expects to be there around 2:30. He's under-promising with the intent to over-deliver. So when he does in fact run into traffic and crazed Bieberettes, he's covered (and not in lava). He got there at 2:55. When you arrive promptly at three, he is sitting there with a hot cup of coffee waiting for you. Impressive!

In both scenarios, the end result was the same, but the expectation was different. In the first scenario, you're upset. In the second, you're thrilled. And the only difference was the application of UPOD.

When you under-promise, or even just need to change the terms, clients will feel a tinge of disappointment. You aren't promising them the world after all, but when delivered the right way, this minor letdown is only temporary and not severe. I call this the Tinge Factor. But you can overcome it by wowing them with UPOD—promising to be there at 3:00, but getting there at 2:55. You're waiting with a cup of coffee, a smile on your face.

The "running late" scenario happens every minute of every day, and it sucks. It's my number-one pet peeve—I always, *always* under-promise and over-deliver. And now you have a strategy to do the same, to wow your clients. Just make a commitment to under-promise ("I'll be there at 3:00") and over-deliver (arrive at 2:55) and you will impress the bejeezus outta everyone.

You're probably used to being overextended. How could you not be, with all of those clients and the neverending cycle of sell–deliver? No matter how good their intentions, no matter how determined they are to make good on promises, overextended entrepreneurs inevitably drop the ball.

Maybe you miss deadlines. Maybe you cut corners so you *can* make deadlines and end up delivering less-than-perfect work. Maybe you make mistakes because you're too exhausted to do your best work. Or maybe you're just always arriving thirty minutes late. No matter what the reason, to your clients, this is unacceptable. You have pissed them off.

Most struggling entrepreneurs scramble for money and time, and because in the past (pre–Pumpkin Plan) you've said yes to working with almost everyone, I'll bet you were scrambling, too. Not anymore. You've killed off the scrawny, diseased clients who sucked up your time and resources. You've committed to nurturing your top clients. You've hopped off the hamster wheel and stopped taking virtually any job that comes your way. You're ready. You can do this. You can dazzle your clients with early deliveries and bonus work they didn't expect. And they *will* be dazzled.

The Under-Promise, Over-Deliver nurture strategy couldn't be simpler, and it's easy to implement. It works across all industries. Here are some examples (and some tips) you could try:

I. When a client asks for a timeline, figure out how much time you need to complete the project and then add a ten-percent buffer. This could be a few days, or a week, or even a month. Look at your past for clues. Are you typically a few hours behind schedule, or do you tend to need an extra two weeks to complete projects?

If you're selling a product, pad your delivery estimates to allow enough time for you to process the order and to accommodate any delays in shipping. This works doubly well when your AOI is speed and efficiency. Could you imagine a rental-car agency promising you that your car will be ready within five minutes of your arrival (pretty darn good) and then delivering it to you in one minute flat (holy crap-oly, that *is* fast.) Zappos, the now famed shoe (and other stuff) retailer skyrocketed to success by delivering orders much earlier than promised. This generated a heck of a lot of "wows" from delighted clients who felt like someone went out of their way to make them happy.

2. When a client asks for a product or service, build in a little something extra. For example, if you're a personal chef, plan to make an extra dessert (and keep that in mind when you're quoting price so you don't lose your profit to strawberries jubilee). Julie Anderson, a couture costume designer I profiled in *The Toilet Paper*

Entrepreneur, always throws in an extra crown, or bag, or pair of shoes when shipping rental costumes, just in case her clients want to try on one more option . . . free of charge. Give your clients an extra twenty minutes for their coaching call. Do the research for them. Add a few extra roses to the bouquet. Just remember to plan for it, so you have the time and money to cover your over-delivering ways.

The key to successful application of UPOD is to slightly ran-domize it. Over-deliver 90 percent of the time; the remaining 10 percent, get it done exactly on time—which will naturally happen in crunch times. Sometimes lava does pour through the streets. Pompeii, people! Pompeii.

Masters of this process will have the work done well before it's due, and will have the comfort of knowing it's done. Remember those days? No panic. No rushing. No freaking out. You may have not had that since the carefree days of childhood. Well, it's back. And it is about to rock the world of your customers. Managing ex-pectations and exceeding them is the formula for super happy, lifelong customers. It's another big, fat feather in your cap.

UPOD also provides a way for you to protect yourself if the customer changes what he wants once you're on a project. If you've completed a project well in advance but have not yet delivered it to the client, and he contacts you with a new directive, you can simply tell him, "Oh, I was just about to surprise you. I already finished it. Here it is." That way, you won't have to redo your work, unless you renegotiate for changes.

Remember, you will be measured ultimately by your actions, not your words. So when you under-promise and over-deliver, you need to avoid being too consistent. Meet your promise some of the time (in other words, exactly deliver), but over-deliver most of the time. If you always over-deliver, people will come to expect it, and then if you aren't able to over-deliver—even though you under-promised—people will be pissed.

Don't Hide the Secret Sauce

Here's another rule I want you to break: "Hide the secret sauce." Once upon a time, companies thought they needed to guard trade secrets as if they were military intelligence. This was smart, because in the olden days, by shrouding yourself in secrecy, no one could copy you and thus you had a key advantage over everyone else.

But now, thanks to the great equalizer known as the Internet, everything anyone would want to know about anything is out there and accessible in just a few clicks. And I mean anything (apparently, even military intelligence). I recently attended a reunion for my old college fraternity. Before the event, I realized I had forgotten the centuries-old, supersecret handshake and password that no one in the frat ever wrote down (for fear of it being stolen). I figured, what the hell, I'll just Google it. Not only did I find a document about it, I discovered a video demonstrating how to do the handshake! Is nothing sacred?

So what does this mean for you? It means that if your client wants to build his own supersonic jet, she can. If your client wants to learn how to make the best cupcakes on the planet, he can. If your clients want to figure out how to fix their own computers, they can. The info is there.

You are no longer the keeper of the secret sauce recipe. You are the executor. You do it for them. You make it easier. You save them time. You get all the best ingredients and cook it in such a way that the result is nothing short of astonishing. You guarantee that you're the best person to actually build the supersonic jet, bake the cupcakes or fix the computers, even when your clients have access to the knowledge to do it themselves.

We live in a near-no-attention-span world, where we are all so overwhelmed by life that we search for easy solutions, for people who will do things for us, sometimes even *think* for us. Just look at the great outsourcing industry that is New York. From parenting your child to walking the dog, to the *delivery* of fast food (because who in New York has the time to walk down the street to the corner deli?), New York is outsourcing life. New York is the racing heart of this nation, perhaps this world, the extreme version of the rest of us.

Most people don't want DIY—takes too long. People are busy. People are stressed and overcommitted and overloaded with information. They want to drive up to the window, place their order and have dinner in five minutes (or less). They want their children to have a first-rate education, but couldn't teach them algebra if they tried. So they are not likely to abuse your willingness to help and be transparent.

Now, don't be a fool. Don't publicly share stuff that will help your competition. Don't share all of your knowledge. Simply share the knowledge that demonstrates you are knowledgeable.

Put the ingredients to the former secret sauce up on your website for the world to see (you don't have to give them the whole recipe). Post it on YouTube. Make a flyer. Or give a speech about it. Or write a book. (Not sayin', just sayin' . . . yes, I do help companies Pumpkin Plan their business. And while this book contains the entire formula, many entrepreneurs and companies still hire my company to help them do it.) It proves to your clients that you know what you're doing. It shows them how you're different. And it gives them comfort in choosing you because they know what you know. (Secrets make people nervous. Go figure.) Sure, some people may decide to take your information and do it themselves, but most people really don't have the time for DIY—especially when they have their own businesses to run and lives to lead. Ironically, the more information I make public, the more my clients hire me. I build trust with them through sharing my knowledge and my unique perspective. (Remember Immutable Laws and AOI?) We want the DIYers to trust us and the outsource lovers to hire us.

So put it out there, because your clients and prospects will find it on their own, anyway. If they get it from you first, you are trusted first . . . a *big* advantage. A Pumpkin Plan advantage.

It only takes one pound to break the world record

In 2009 Ohioan Christy Harp beat the world record for the largest pumpkin ever grown. It weighed in at 1,725 pounds! (Google Christy so you can see the picture. She's standing behind the pumpkin, so you can't see the bottom half of her body. Seriously, she looks like she could be on *Mystery Diagnosis* or the cover art for a chapter in a medical oddities book: Pumpkin Tumor Gone Wild!) As I write this, Christy still holds the world record, but it could be shattered come October. You see, Christy beat the previous world-record holder, Joe Jutras of Rhode Island, by only thirty-six pounds. His pumpkin weighed in at 1,689 pounds just two years earlier.

It doesn't take much extra effort to beat the world record. Even one pound will do. And it doesn't take much effort to have all your clients see you as their world-class, de facto provider. Even if you are just *that much* better than everyone else . . . you are better than everyone else. And you will get all the rewards. Just a few tweaks in your approach, or systems, or product, or service could be enough to get their attention. I say this because I don't want you to get stuck trying to come up with an elaborate plan to impress your key client group. This ain't Vegas, baby. You don't need dancing girls or dancing fountains. You simply need to be a little bit better, a little bit more helpful, and a little bit more creative at solving problems for your VIPs.

Every Olympic gold medalist is just a little better than the silver medalist. And when you look at the range of scores among these elite athletes, you often find that the gold medalist was only a few points away from last place, too. By the time swimmer Michael Phelps took his turn in the men's 4x100-meter freestyle relay in the 2008 Olympic Games in Beijing, he had already won seven gold medals. Halfway through his 100-meter butterfly he was way behind, seventh to hit the wall. He picked up speed and caught up to the leader, but everyone—including his mom—was stunned when he was declared the winner. He won his eighth consecutive gold medal—and beat Mark Spitz's world record of seven gold medals in one Olympics—by a mere 0.01 seconds.

How did he do this? He reached out and slapped the side of the pool before the other guy did. A hand slap was the difference between gold and silver—0.01 seconds. (Okay, it was technically a half-stroke, but it sure looked like a hand slap to me.)

You probably know the name Michael Phelps. Do you know

the other guy's name? The guy who lost to Michael Phelps by nothing more than a high-five? Didn't think so.

Just a little better gets you the Wheaties box. A little bit less and you're "that other guy" no one can remember.

Amazing is just one pound heavier and one second faster than everyone else, and it's not that hard to work your way up to amazing. For now, do the easy thing, the simple thing. Do the thing that you can do *right now*. You just added lots of pounds to your pumpkin . . . easy. If your competitor typically delivers projects in five days, deliver yours in four. If your competitor has a super hot sauce, make a super, *super* hot sauce. If your competitor has a ten-year warranty, make yours twelve.

You don't have to grow a pumpkin as large as a house to nab the world record. You only need one pound.

Work the Plan—
Take Action in 30 Minutes (or Less)

I. *Develop a "favorite client" policy.* I drop everything for my favorite clients. I'll take a call from my top client even if I'm already on a call with a different, lower-tier client. Take a few moments to figure out how your business will treat your key client group like VIPs. Make that policy very clear to your team and start implementing it immediately.

2. *Create systems to implement the Under-Promise, Over-Deliver strategy.* Looking at your current projects, products or services, how could you set up an under-promise for them with the smallest Tinge Factor? Then figure out how to over-deliver on them. What extra little something could you do to wow your clients? Then, look at the repeat services you provide and come up with a new timetable that enables you to under-promise.

How to Pumpkin Plan Your Industry — Manufacturing

Let's pretend you own a brewery—yes, I know it's a dream come true, but I need you to put the drink *down* and focus. We're going to Pumpkin Plan your industry.

You brew beer out of a medium-sized building, and you have a small foothold in the regional microbrewery market, which is super competitive. You try to get the main distributor to push your beer. But he makes his money selling all the big name brands, so even though you really don't have much of a margin, you have to do the only thing you can that will catch the distributor's attention—slash your prices. At first, orders pick up and you're busier than ever—not much profit rolling in, but you figure it'll all even out in the end.

Except for this one little problem: you can't *keep* slashing your prices. There's just no room. So when five of your biggest competitors cut prices again, you're screwed. Suddenly, the new customers drop off, the distributor drops you and you're left with your old standby restaurants and bars, who now pay a lower price for the same beer.

So you decide to Pumpkin Plan your business. You begin by filling out the Assessment Chart, identifying your top customers (whom you now refer to as clients, thank you very much). With all of the new, bargain-hunting clients gone, you really don't have to fire anyone, so you focus on getting to know your best clients better.

Normally you rely on your restaurants to push your products, so you really don't have much of a relationship with your clients. So when you call them up and ask if you could meet with them, they're welcoming. When you interview them, you realize that they are true fans of your beer, but they really wish that your industry would work more closely with them to create beers exclusively for their restaurants.

You go back to your team with this little tidbit, and together you realize that this fits your particular sweet spot perfectly. Your top clients want to create exclusive beers with you, you love creating new flavors—and you're really damn good at it—and once you do create a new beer, it's easy for you to replicate it over and over again. So you go back to your top clients with your new collaborative program, and ask their opinion about it. They give you a few helpful suggestions, you tweak your program, and when they say, "When can we get started?" you know you're on to something.

Within six months you've created five new beers—one for each of your top clients. Your clients are thrilled. They enjoyed the creative process and they can't get over the fact that they have their *own* beer. So they push the beer, and soon you're selling more of your new beer than any of your old labels. So you minimize production on the other, low-profit-margin beer and cut related expenses.

Then, something you could never have imagined starts to happen. Orders for your beer from the restaurants go up 400 percent. Why, you ask? The restaurants are not only giving the beer prime placement in their menus, they are also encouraging customers to buy six-packs to take home with their doggy bags. One restaurant has paired their food with your beer on the menu. Amazing! It used to be beer (or wine) pairings to the food . . . this place is actually doing the opposite with your customized beer.

Eventually, you figure out how to systematize the collaboration process, so that now you can work with other restaurants around the country to create exclusive beers for their patrons. You start charging a collaboration fee, and you split the profits with your top clients.

Because you've mastered the process, you get a reputation for being an excellent collaborator, and now you're getting requests from restaurants in other countries—from event planners looking for an edge for their biggest parties, from corporations looking for interesting incentives. You're making exclusive beers to help promote movies. You've got deals with major restaurant chains. You're the go-to company for creating site- and event-specific beer—and you have the bulging bank account to show for it.

CHAPTER EIGHT

THE WISH LIST

Remember John Shaw, the solar guy from Colorado? As you know, John's a giant, solar panel–installin' Pumpkin Planner in a really, *really* saturated field. His business went through the roof (pun intended) when he stopped installing solar hot water systems—effectively killing off the clients who, through no fault of their own, seriously ate up his time *and* dipped into his profit margin. But that wasn't the end of John's stellar growing season. John supersized his business when he figured out what frustrated his prospects the most . . . and then did something about it.

John knew that in Durango, there were two different government rebate programs for people who switched over to solar energy, and that these saved clients around $6,000 on the installation of a system that could cost upwards of $25,000. He knew that many prospective clients wanted to install solar panels, but they just couldn't swing it because they didn't have the upfront cash.

John listened carefully to his clients and prospects, asked questions, took note of their frustrations with his industry, and then did some recon. He'd long paid attention to other solar installers in other parts of the country where solar energy was even more common. After a bit of research he discovered how some solar companies in Northern California expanded their market beyond their wealthy clientele and made solar energy accessible to people who wouldn't normally be able to afford it. John decided to try it out in Colorado.

Here is a little pumpkin-farming magic: If it works for another farmer, it almost always works for you. And if it works for you one time, it almost always works for you a second time. John got this, so when he saw rebate financing working in another market, he was confident it would also work in his. It was a no-brainer.

John had $50,000 or so in cash reserves, and realized he could probably float the $6,000 for some clients until the rebates came in, effectively solving the cash-poor problem many prospects complained about. "I started giving clients temporary loans based on the total amount they would get back from state and local rebate programs," John explained to me. "It only takes a few months to get the rebates. I fill out all of the paperwork and I have the rebate check sent straight to me, so there's no real risk."

Genius. Pure Pumpkin Planning genius.

By paying attention to the concerns, wishes and frustrations of his clients and prospects, John was able to spot an amazing opportunity to wow them and expand his business like crazy. He was able to reach a whole new group of clients who, though top-client material in almost every other way, weren't liquid enough to pay for John's pricey service.

The big news here is, John didn't have to spend months brainstorming how to solve this problem, nor did he spend years testing things out. He simply discovered the concerns and frustrations his clients shared and listened closely to their wishes, so that when opportunities presented themselves, the right choice was obvious. You see, a Pumpkin Planner's success is not in having better answers . . . it is in asking better questions, better defining the problem. When you do this, the answers present themselves. The answer, the *best* answer, is obvious.

John's clients feel special, like he's advocating for them, taking care of them, going the extra mile for them . . . because he *is*. And all of that innovation and nurturing helped John grow the biggest pumpkin in town.

One of the single most effective strategies I use as part of my own Pumpkin Plan is something I call the "Wish List." I interview my top clients to find out what they wish they could change about my industry, what they wish I could do for them or sell to them, what they wish someone—anyone—could solve for them, what would make their jobs so much easier, what would help them grow their business. Then, I do my best to play fairy godfather and fulfill every possible wish.

For example, at Olmec, my first company, we billed hourly. When we interviewed our top clients, several said, "We have no idea what you do; we don't understand it. So we have no idea if this is a fair price." That's when we switched to a flat monthly rate, and our clients were thrilled. When we billed hourly, they had no idea how to compare us to other computer-services companies, or determine if it would be cheaper for them to just hire someone to work with them in-house. They couldn't figure it out because they weren't really sure what we did, and quite frankly, they really didn't want to know. They just wanted their computers fixed. But with the new flat-rate billing they were able to do a cost analysis in, oh, about two minutes. "Hey, if we hire someone to work in-house, to do whatever the hell Olmec does, it will cost $75,000, but if we keep our contract with Olmec, it will only cost $45,000."

Now, you can't be everything to everyone . . . you have to go back to the good ol' sweet spot diagram to see if it makes sense to fulfill the wish.

The Wish List is like a map to buried treasure. Behind every complaint and crazy, "impossible" ask, there is an opportunity to innovate, differentiate and ultimately dominate your industry. Rather than ignore his less-affluent prospects, John listened, came up with a solution to their major problem (innovate), became the only solar panel company that provided the solution to the problem (differentiate) and went on to corner the middle-class market (dominate).

The key to explosive growth is competing reasonably well in every area your competition competes in, and then blowing them away in one category. It is really that simple. Be "in the ball park" for everything you do, except for one thing. For that one thing, swing for the fences. Be one pound bigger. Solve one key problem. Be one second faster than everyone else. Do this, and to your clients you are the only choice, the gold-medal standard. Your client's Wish List is your secret weapon in this endeavor.

The client interview

Don't be surprised if most of your clients are totally shocked when you ask them what's on their Wish List. This isn't the typical vendor "feedback" call. You know the one I'm talking about—a sales rep calls you up to find out "how they're doing" but either doesn't really listen to you, or you get to the end of the call and realize they just wasted your time so they could pitch you something. Or my favorite, when the person who just helped you says, "I have a satisfaction survey that will occur at the end of the call and I want to make sure I get a five-star rating . . . did I deliver five-star service?" I mean, come on! Don't try your stupid mind voodoo on me. Here's what I want that jackhole to understand: If you have to ask if you delivered five-star service, guess what? You didn't!

Even on the rare occasions when this guy seems genuinely to want your feedback, nine times out of nine (yeah, do the math), he won't act on it afterward.

A Pumpkin Plan "feedback" call isn't really a feedback call at all. You're not even going to ask your clients about how you could serve them better—because they're probably not going to articulate it, anyway. Whatever they do tell you will amount to watered-down half-truths, because let's face it, most people would rather spare your feelings and avoid confrontation than tell you what they really think. Or they will be confused, because they haven't yet imagined how you could serve them better. If you go in to the client interviews asking them to "rate your performance," you're going to get mostly high marks, a fifteen-minute conversation and a handshake.

The Wish List is not about you—how *you* can improve, how awesome *you* are. The Wish list is about your clients, and what they need to grow their own giant pumpkin.

When you interview your clients, ask questions about your industry, not your company. Ask questions about their aspirations, challenges, short-term and long-term goals. Ask questions that will help you learn more about their business and their industry *beyond* what directly affects your company. To get you started, here are a few questions I use in client interviews:

1. What is your chief complaint about your industry? Your clients? Other vendors?

2. If you could do it easily, what would you change about your industry? Your clients? Other vendors?

3. What is your biggest challenge right now?

4. What would need to change so you could finish work an hour earlier every day?

5. What would you like to accomplish in the near future?

6. Where do you hope to be in five years? Ten? Twenty?

7. What frustrates you about vendors in *my* industry? What do you wish vendors in my industry would do differently?

8. If you could tweak the products or services my industry provides to better suit your needs, what would you change?

9. What is most confusing about my industry?

10. What do you wish vendors in my industry *would* offer?

Remember, your job is not to sell your clients on anything, or even promise them that you will come up with the solutions to their problems. You just want to get to know them better, to understand what they're all about. You're just looking for the seedlings of ideas . . . stuff for you to ruminate on and then find that key solution that will take you to the next level. As you interview multiple top clients, you are looking for trends or common themes in their requests and complaints. For now, just be appreciative of their time and insight, 'cause you have a lot of thinking to do tonight. Move on to the next client and ask the same questions, look for the patterns, and fix them!

With the answers to these (and any other questions you can dream up), you now have Wish Lists for your clients. Again, this is like gold, because if you can defy their imagination and solve a crucial problem for them, they will love you—and do business with you—for a long, long time.

Ask Better Questions

Your brain is always working to find an answer, a solution to the questions you pose. This happens at a subconscious level. You ask a question of yourself, and your brain starts plugging away automatically. Then, usually at the most inconvenient times—like when you are in the shower and, I presume, without pen and paper—the answer pops into your mind. You have been working on it, seeking it, in the deep, dark regions of your brain, and then it works its way out suddenly, unexpectedly. Kinda like that surprise Snickers bar from this past Halloween that you find sandwiched between your couch cushions. You never saw it coming. But whammo, there it is. And it's delightful.

The key here is that your brain goes to work on any question you ask it. Good, bad or indifferent . . . your brain keeps plugging away. You need to be very aware of the questions you ask yourself, because the quality of your question will directly influence the quality of your answer.

If you ask, "Why do I always struggle?" your brain will answer: "Because you suck." Okay, usually your brain comes up with specific answers, like "Because you're not well-educated," or "Because you don't have enough money," or "Because you're not good at sales."

Conversely, if you ask, "How do I achieve success?" your brain will come back with an answer: "Try this, do that . . ." If you consistently ask enabling questions, your brain will find enabling answers—solutions toward progress. Pumpkin Planners consistently ask better questions, get better answers and, ultimately, get better results.

I started my current company, Obsidian Launch, with the intent to help new companies launch. That focus morphed into behavioral web design—helping companies launch their products and services so that they take off explosively—because I kept asking, "What can I offer my clients that would have the biggest impact and give them the most benefit, and that would be easy for me to replicate?" Because I asked better and better questions of myself, I attracted better clients. I went from working with exhausted, desperate entrepreneurs who could neither afford me nor put in the time and work necessary for success to working with striving, focused entrepreneurs looking to take a product, a service or their entire company to the next level.

Be very aware of your self-talk. Ask better questions. Ask bigger questions. And you will get better, bigger results.

COULD I GET A LITTLE ADVICE, PLEASE?

When you've developed something new in response to something on your clients' Wish List, your next step is to find out if you're on point. Rather than offer the product or service for sale, ask for advice. Call up your top clients and say, "I'm trying to improve my services/product, and I'm not sure if I'm there yet. I don't know what I don't know. I have nothing to offer or to sell. May I buy you a cup of coffee and simply get some advice from you? It won't take longer than fifteen minutes."

This strategy works because you're telling them, "I see you as an authority, someone with valuable knowledge." And that, my friend, is irresistible to most folks. Hot diggity dog, you are calling on clients for advice. They love to be perceived as experts (we all do), and when you are genuinely looking for guidance—and not trying to sell them *anything,* and I do mean anything—you make them feel all happy and important inside. And best of the best part, you get crucial feedback about your product or service . . . drum roll . . . from your clients! If it's not workin' for them, you'll know, because they won't ask you for more information. It's really that simple—if clients are into your idea, they'll ask you to follow up, or they'll ask how much it costs . . . they'll pursue you. If they don't, then just thank them for their time and go back to the drawing board.

Before he started his business, Scott Weintraub had a pretty good idea of what his prospects' Wish List looked like. He and his business partner, Jeffrey Spanbauer, decided to leave the corporate world after years working in brand management and marketing for the pharmaceutical industry, so they knew all about the challenges major pharmaceutical companies faced with respect to marketing and sales.

"If you're a product director or VP of marketing for a pharmaceutical company, you are typically frustrated by the variation in your product's performance," Scott explained to me at his beach house one day. "You might get twenty percent of the market in

Boston, five percent in Dallas, two percent in St. Louis . . . lots of variation. This is especially frustrating when you're marketing drugs that bring in five hundred million dollars. You say, 'If we could just fix Dallas, oh my gosh!' But you're not sure *how* to fix Dallas, so you use the same marketing approach and tools for the whole country."

While at Pfizer, Scott and Jeff tried to start a regional marketing division to address the problem, but it didn't fly. So when they were laid off after cutbacks, they decided to start their own company. With the help of a wizard of a mathematician, they developed a proprietary process that tells pharmaceutical companies what the biggest driver of performance is in every single territory in the country. (See what a little nerd power can get ya?)

"Most companies have around one hundred territories," Scott explains. "So now we can tell you that in Boston, you need the cardiologists' influence with family doctors. In L.A., you need to work on the price of your drug. In Chicago, it's all about spending time with your most important doctors. In Atlanta, you have to focus on the African American patients." Exact same product. Different marketing approach in each city.

Sounds like a winner, right? A bona fide Atlantic Giant seed. It was, but what I really love about this story is how Scott and Jeff took their *own* wish list, and then went back to their colleagues to get their advice about the product. They shared it with two dozen brand marketers—people they knew, and others who had been referred to them by people they knew.

"I talked to my friends and ex-coworkers and said, 'I have this idea for a company, what parts would help you, and what parts don't matter?' I showed them a standard PowerPoint presentation, and asked for their feedback. They would say, 'Change this, clarify that,' so we kept refining it and going back out for more advice. Finally, I showed it to a friend of a friend who said, 'This is really good. How much does it cost?' That's when we knew we had something."

How much does it cost? Those are the magic, golden words, my friend.

When a client or prospect asks, "How much does it cost," you know they want what you're offering. Now, you can really kick your new innovation into high gear.

Here's the part of the story where things really took off for Scott and Jeff. Scott says, "So Jeff tells me his friend Will told him to call this guy Seth, here's his number. So I call Seth and say, 'I'm thinking of starting this company, and Will said I should give you a call, that you may have some advice for me. Can I stop by and show you what I'm thinking?' "

I love this story so much, I am on the verge of blurting out the ending to you. But I am trying to hold it in. Don't . . . want . . . to . . . ruin . . . it . . . for . . . you.

Seth's assistant calls Scott back. ("This should have been a clue," Scott says.) The assistant gives him his options—Tuesday or Thursday—and asks in which office he would like the meeting to take place, Brunswick or Bridgewater? ("This *also* should have been a clue," Scott says, chuckling.)

I . . . can . . . barely . . . resist . . . telling . . . you . . .

On the day of the appointment, Scott arrives at the Johnson & Johnson building. He takes the elevator up, and as soon as he enters the lobby, he realizes he's in the executive suite. "The carpet pile's higher, and the wood-grain paneling is really made out of wood. This is the real deal. Again, this should have been a clue. She walks me down to his office, introduces me to Seth, who hands me his business card. It reads, 'Seth Fischer, Chairman of Pharmaceuticals, Johnson & Johnson.' "

Yup. *Chairman.* Until Scott shook Seth's hand, he had no idea he was meeting with a big cheese—so big, his "yes" could change everything for Scott and Jeff.

How does the story end?

With all kinds of awesome, that's how. I'll let Scott blurt it out to you . . .

"I get five slides into my presentation and Seth says, 'Do you mind if I call in the VP of Marketing? I think he'd be interested in this.' So he picks up the phone and says, 'Hey, Bob, this is Seth. Can you come over to my office?' When Bob walks in, Seth says, 'Bob, this is my *friend*, Scott, and he has something you'd really be interested in. Scott, do you mind starting over?' I get up to slide five and Bob says, 'Seth, this is exactly what we've been talking about. Where did you find this guy?' I go through five more slides, and finally Bob says, 'Can you come back and meet with two of our brand teams? They *need* this.' And that's when it hit me: we're on to something. This really resonates with people who can make key buying decisions."

Scott and Jeff got right on it and launched Healthcare Regional Marketing.

In the first three days they landed $500,000 in contracts with Johnson & Johnson and two other major pharmaceutical companies.

In their second year of business, they brought in $4 million.

Last year, their fourth, they grossed $14.2 million.

First, Scott and Jeff intuited their prospects' Wish List based on their own experiences working for those companies. Then, they created a product that solved the market variation problem all pharmaceutical companies experienced. And then they sought advice from colleagues and their colleagues' friends, until they had a product that excited prospects so much, they wanted to buy it right on the spot . . . without Scott and Jeff having to sell it to them.

Are you with me? Let's say it together . . . genius.

One more time.

Genius.

It's all about the label

Consumers use labels to quickly qualify what they're buying. If your clients label your business in the same way they label your competition, they might as well stick a fork in you . . . 'cause you're done. When your label is the same as your competition's, that means your client or prospect can hardly tell the difference between the two of you—if she can at all. You probably do this yourself, applying generic labels to vendors you hire. A cable guy is a cable guy. An auto mechanic is an auto mechanic. A broker, a business coach, a lawyer, a whatever . . . these are all labels. These labels put you in a generic category, making it easy for clients and prospects to quickly understand what you do. The problem is, they put you in the same category as your competitors. To your client, you are just the same as the good ones, the bad ones and the pathetic ones. And when a customer defines you by a preestablished label, they have a pre-defined set of ideas about what that means.

Let me give you an example of expert labeling. What do you call the guy or gal who fixes your computer? I have a clever name for mine—I call him "the computer guy." (Yes, you may steal that one.) There are plenty of computer guys out there, and plenty of businesses where you can go to hire one. And then there's Best Buy's Geek Squad. The Geek Squad is, at its heart, nothing more than a team full of computer guys and gals, but that's not how their customers think of them. Their customers think of them as geeks. What's in a name, you ask? Everything. By using the word "geek" in their company name, Best Buy differentiates its computer-repair guys and gals from everyone else's. They're not just average guys; they're geeks, nerds, *experts—masters*. And, by using the word "squad" in their name, the geeks indicate that they are able respond quickly because they are members of an organized force.

But the image doesn't stop with the name. The Geek Squad backs up its labeling with presentation—the geeks are dressed in floodwater pants; they have pens in their pockets; they drive VW bugs painted to look like a police (squad) car. In this way they emphasize the idiosyncrasies they point out in their name. If you're looking for just any "computer guy," you'll probably end up choosing the cheapest option. Why pay more for Joe at Acme Computer Guys to debug some software if the teenage computer guy next door can do the same thing for a six-pack of beer that he can't buy himself? But if you have an urgent computer issue, like a DEFCON #1 life-or-death kind of computer issue, you don't want the teenager next door or the retired guy who only worked on mainframes; you want a super-advanced, grade-A, Underoos-wearing nerd to come to the rescue. Comparing one computer guy to another is like comparing apples to apples. Comparing a computer guy to the Geek Squad is like comparing Inspector Gadget to James Bond. When I'm in a panic, I'll take rescue nerd. Every time, no matter what it costs.

If you're labeled as a computer guy, your prospect is thinking you are just the same as everyone else. "I already have a computer guy, and I'm sticking with him, unless this new guy (that's you) can give me a better deal." After all, you're both computer guys, right? This is why so often, the choice between you and your competition comes down to price.

You could argue a million ways to Sunday that the other computer guy is better than the Geek Squad. I should know; with Olmec I was the other computer guy . . . and I was better because I could handle more complex stuff. But my customers didn't care. The customer doesn't have years or decades to understand your craft the way you do. So as a customer, you look for the obvious and easy-to-understand differences. You make a decision, often, on less than one percent of the information, because you have to. If you want to communicate your differences quickly to customers, change your label. Don't cram yourself in with all the other guys.

If you can get your clients and prospects to label you differently—not just for the *sake* of being different, but because you *are* different—you make it easy for clients to notice your differences . . . and to choose you over the competition. Oh—and if you do a good enough job, price becomes irrelevant, so you can charge more than the other guys and finally earn what you are really worth.

When Scott and Jeff set out to form their own company, they knew that if they labeled themselves "marketing experts" for pharmaceutical companies, they would just be seen as one in a vast sea of consulting firms. So they took their industry's main frustration, found a solution and turned that into their differentiator. When they opened their doors, they were "regional marketing experts," with little or no competition because they had a new label. They knew they could be good marketing consultants, or they could be the best damn *regional* marketing consultants in the country. And I think $14.2 million in four years, says heck, yes, they got it right.

In the same way, John Shaw is not just another "solar energy guy." John is the equal opportunity solar-energy provider. He makes it possible for nearly everyone in his community who wants solar energy to get it. He turned his clients' chief frustration (lack of upfront cash) into a solution. Since he started facilitating the rebate system for his clients and financing their down payments, Shaw Solar has secured more than $250,000 in rebates and grants for his clients. This is John's differentiator.

See how your clients' Wish List could lead to further refinement of your niche, and to the discovery of a lucrative differentiator? Good. I knew you were paying attention.

You won't have the capability, or the desire, to fulfill every item on your clients' Wish List. That's okay. Actually, that's more than okay because you only have to be the world's best at one thing in order to have clients flocking to you. Your goal is to work within your sweet spot, not outside of your comfort zone. Not every good business idea is a great idea for *your business*.

That said, you sure could use the Wish List to watch out for ways to heap loads of love and awesomeness on to your top clients. If you know what their aspirations and frustrations are, you're better equipped to spot opportunities for them. It doesn't always have to be your company that solves the problem—hook them up whenever you find something that will help them. Be invested in their success. Be amazing. Rock their world. The love that you give them will come back.

Work the Plan—
Take Action in 30 Minutes (or Less)

I. *Draw up your own list of interview questions.* Using my list for inspiration, create your own list of questions to ask clients when you sit down to interview them. What do you really want to know about them? Remember to keep the focus 100 percent on them, not you. Never ask direct questions about your company's performance (it is unlikely they will tell you the God's honest truth); ask questions about your industry as a whole. No sales questions or leading questions! Let them speak their minds . . . there's gold in them there brains.

2. *Look for commonalities and innovate.* After you interview several top clients, look for commonalities in their Wish Lists. Do they share similar frustrations about their own industry? Are they all looking for a solution to the same problem? If you can find a way to solve it, or make all of their lives easier and their businesses more profitable, well then, I'd say you're in like Flynn.

3. *Get some advice.* If you decide to create a new product or offer a new service that could ease the frustrations of your top clients, call them up again and ask them for their advice. Never launch a new offering without getting feedback from your clients *first*. If they love it, they'll tell you . . . without you even needing to ask. If they think it needs work, they'll tell you. If they see no value in it, they'll be polite and never ask you about it again. So it will be easy for you to figure out if your new offering is ready for a test drive. It's all about asking advice.

How to Pumpkin Plan Your Industry — Tech Services

Let's pretend you're a web designer—not the geeky kind, but the super-hip kind with three Tumblr accounts and an impressive iTunes collection. So put down your fair-trade coffee, shut down your Mac and let's Pumpkin Plan your business.

You're a freelance web designer with about two dozen ongoing clients. You work sixteen-hour days, six days a week, and pass out on Sundays. The money is decent, but you can't let up because you never know when a client will drop or postpone a project. So you keep saying yes to new clients, adding more and more work to your insanely huge pile, figuring it will all even out eventually . . . hopefully before you die.

After you fill out your Assessment Chart, you realize you have maybe four top clients, and at least ten crappy clients who just have to go. You fire the worst of the bunch, and have the happy realization that this Pumpkin Plan stuff really works when your income actually jumps immediately. You have more time to work with the better, higher-paying clients and they take you up on your availability. But, you know there is some more cutting to do. For that you will wait until after you interview your top clients, thinking maybe you'll find the *best* way to free yourself from the remaining diseased clients after you get a handle on your top clients' Wish Lists.

Turns out, your top clients are all companies that have extensive websites with integrated social media and storefronts. When you sit down for the interview, you learn that their biggest frustration is having to constantly upload all of the new content themselves—they're just too busy.

Going back to your list of eight remaining diseased clients, you notice that they are all pretty much DIY, small-scale clients. So you opt to eliminate services for companies looking to just "put something up" and then manage it themselves. Because let's face it—they may *think* they're DIY, but they're absolutely *not* DIY. They call and email you all the time with questions and problems, and because you're such a nice person, you just answer them. Well, not anymore!

With your low-paying, high-maintenance clients gone, you focus on providing stellar, we-do-it-for-you service for your top clients. You establish a monthly retainer, rather than an hourly rate, which they are happy to pay just for the privilege of not having to figure anything out or worry about how much it will cost to have you "just do it." Then, you hire a few upstarts on a part-time, as-needed basis to help you with the easy stuff, and spend your time and energy on a strategic web design and maintenance plan for each client, managing clients and working the rest of the Pumpkin Plan.

Now, even with your little helpers, you have more money, fewer headaches and more time to spend enjoying your life (what a concept).

You reach out to your top clients and ask for vendor referrals. When you talk with a representative from the merchant services company who runs the credit card transactions for two of your top clients, you discover that their biggest beef with all of their clients (including your mutual clients) is the way they set up the ordering forms on their website. It seems that just a few tweaks would help prevent lost and error-ridden transactions, which cost the merchant services company money *and* aggravate your client. So you come up with a new form that meets both of their needs. The people at the merchant services company are so happy, they send out an email blast to their entire client database, urging them to contact you about setting up proper forms on their own websites. Soon enough, you're swimming in inquiries, and have your pick of clients.

Next, you get started on your UPOD. First, you promise to give them a very basic monthly traffic report for their website—just the basic summary of the days' activities. Nothing fancy. Then, you surprise them with a free, detailed monthly performance report that identifies who buys what, when and from where, and even recommends which products they should focus on promoting next month. The clients are big-time wowed and the cash just keeps rolling in.

CHAPTER NINE

LET THEM LEAD

What if you could predict, within a small margin of error, exactly how many people would buy your new product or sign up for your new service? What if you could build a community committed to promoting your new product or service before you even finished developing it? What if you could be sure that every time—and I do mean *every time*—you launch a new product or service, you absolutely, positively knew it would not fail?

Screw the "what ifs."

Because you totally can.

The process is pretty straightforward. No mystery, no hocus-pocus, no nonsense. You simply need to get your customer community to directly influence the development, launch and marketing of your offering. At the end of this process, you'll have a product your clients already want (because they built it for themselves), and the rest of the strategy will take care of itself. I call this the "Insider Strategy" because it gives your clients insider access to the goings-on of your company, and you get insider access to their minds. This is co-creation at its most effective. And just as the sun handles the vast majority of the responsibility of growing pumpkins, or any life for that matter, the community of these clients, prospects and vendors acts as the sun for your business—giving it the energy it needs to grow and grow and grow. Let the sun shine, baby!

The Insider Strategy is about more than just figuring out a way to market your product. There are several other benefits to acting on this idea:

- It breeds innovation in product development: As you become more connected to the needs, wants and ideas of your community, you create new products or services that you may not have thought of without their input.

- It saves you money. Because you can predict how a product or service will sell, you can save yourself from developing and marketing something that no one really wants, or modify your offering until they do want it.

- It shapes your brand. As you get to know your community by letting them become insiders, you gain a better understanding of what your brand means to them—why they love you, what you represent, why they keep coming back.

- It inspires loyalty. When clients participate in the creation of a product or service, they feel important, *significant*. And when people feel significant *because of your company*, they will be loyal for life—or at least until they stop feeling that way.

- It motivates unsolicited promotion. Your insiders will ultimately promote the products or services they helped create. The conversation they have with friends is no longer "Look how cool this thing is that this *company* made." It changes to "Look how cool this thing is that *I* made."

Let me just throw one caveat into my "simple plan" declaration: If you're not working the *rest* of the Pumpkin Plan, this strategy will not work well for you. In fact, it could totally fail, and drive you nuts in the process. It could fail because—and this is *key*, my fellow Pumpkin Planner—as long as you're catering to every type of client under the sun (instead of nurturing only your top clients); as long as you're spinning plates in your jack-of-all-trades costume (instead of focusing on a tight niche and building your team around it); as long as you're grasping at straws (instead of planting your own Atlantic Giant seed), implementing the Insider Strategy will lead you down divergent paths, all ending at one place: Crazytown, aka the bankruptcy capital of the world.

I know this sounds harsh, but it's true. When you put the cart before the horse, bad things happen. So promise me you won't use this strategy until you're rockin' the other steps of the Pumpkin Plan.

Deal?

Deal.

Okay, now that we have an understanding, let's get down to it . . .

CROWDSOURCING PLUS

I'm pretty sure you know all about crowdsourcing, but just in case you've never heard of it, crowdsourcing is what happens when you use a large external group (that is, not your own staff) to facilitate an objective, whether it be to develop a product, launch an initiative or simply complete a task. A crowd can be used to map the universe and the gazillions of galaxies within it (Galaxy Zoo), disseminate local information at lightning speed (Twitter), conduct complex disease research (Fold.It), and it can be used to generate content for blogs or books (*Chuck Norris Cannot Be Stopped: 400 All-New Facts about the Man Who Knows Neither Fear nor Mercy . . .* and other timeless classics).

And it can be used to build a $30 million-plus company. The T-shirt company Threadless is a popular example of crowdsourcing done right. Launched in 2000 with $1,000 in seed money, Threadless lets the people who buy their stuff (their *clients*) design their stuff, too.

The company asks designers to create their own T-shirt designs, one of which is selected as Threadless's next T-shirt. The result is an amped-up base who are psyched to be allowed to create the next great product they're going to buy. And the winner of the contest? Well, that person is a loyal Threadless customer for life. When people say, "Hey, where'd you buy that cool T-shirt?" she'll say, "Buy it? I *made* this mother-effer!" And you know, because she's vested in this process, she's promoting the T-shirt (and Threadless) all over her town . . . and her Tumblr blog . . . and her Facebook page . . . and her Twitter feed. Once people get involved in the development of a new product or service, they become loyal toward it and want to promote it. In fact, they really can't *help themselves*. They want the world to know that they have participated in creating something new, that they are connected to a company they *already* thought was really cool.

Threadless produces a sick amount of revenue and a sick amount of profit from crowdsourcing. When they offer a new

T-shirt design, they sell out. One hundred percent. Not one measly T-shirt left, not even in a random box in the back of the warehouse. They're all gone. Who else can say that? When was the last time you sold out of something? When was the last time you maxed out your availability?

Still, while crowdsourcing is an amazingly effective tool for garnering client loyalty and inspiring enthusiastic participation in marketing your products or services, the Insider Strategy will rock your world. The main difference is predictability. When you crowdsource a product or service, you can't really be sure whether it will catch fire or perform weakly and fizzle out, because you haven't necessarily involved the "crowd" from the inception of your idea.

The Insider Strategy allows you to measure client responsiveness right from the get-go and at every stage of the process. And since early behaviors are big indicators of what's to come, you'll know if a new offering will succeed or fail before you put any effort into developing it. You'll know because the very first thing you're going to say is not, "Go ahead and send us your best designs (ideas)" but rather, "I have this idea for X. Is this something you would be interested in?"

It's a simple distinction, but it makes all the difference because it is a predictor of your success or failure. A "no" response tells you that people don't want what you have to offer. Period. Bummer, but at least now you know, right? At least you're not sweating over the creation of a new product or service that nobody will ever want. Asking if people would be interested in what you're *thinking* about offering before you actually invest in developing it saves you gobs of time, money and effort.

No answer at all is better defined as the silence before the silence. If your core customers don't respond immediately, that's a big sign that your offering won't sell and that you don't have enough rapport with your community. If you don't have at least a small group of clients interested in your offering, this is an absolutely clear indicator that you have not properly tilled your pumpkin patch. A collection of "Yes, I'm interested" responses points to a pending success.

After you've tried the predictor stage a few times—and meticulously recorded the client responses—you'll be able to predict how many sales you'll end up with. Really. For example, I know that if I am selling a product that costs $100 or less, I will get a thirty-nine-percent purchase rate. So, if 500 people respond to my predictor question with a resounding "yes," I know I'll most likely sell 195 units of whatever I'm selling.

Using the Insider Strategy is *so* going to change your life—and help you grow, grow, grow. Why?

One reason is that when you can predict how many people will buy what you're selling, you don't have to build, create, order or buy more than you need. No more sagging cardboard boxes stuffed with last year's products. No more wasted hours brainstorming a new type of service no one will want. No more spending money you don't have to build something no one really wants.

When people respond positively to your offering, they're locked in right from the beginning. So as you move through the Insider Strategy process, most of them stay with you, and eventually purchase whatever *they said they wanted*, as soon as it becomes available. So now you've got built-in sales, with little or no marketing dollars spent to get them.

And, when people get involved in helping you develop your new product or service, *and if you give them credit*, they become very invested in the outcome, so much so that they will promote your new offering—even if you never ask them to do so! So you have a built-in "street team" spreading the word about your launch. (And they're doing it for free. Do you get me?!? For *free*.)

Because you have the Wish List, you can add another layer to the early predictor stage by asking clients, "In response to your wish (or complaint, concern, frustration), I'm working on X. Would this fit the bill? Would you be interested in this?" Now you *really* have vested clients, because they inspired the idea in the first place. And let me tell you, inspiring someone else to innovate is irresistible to most people—it's like crack! Except even if you're addicted to it, it won't ruin your life. Subtle difference.

Are you jumping up and down yet? Is your mind racing with possibilities? Are you starting to see how using this marketing method could really help you bring home the blue ribbon?

Fantastic.

A CULT FOLLOWING

Despite his low-key workshop and his small crew (seriously, he's practically a one-man band), Paul Scheiter of Hedgehog Leather-works is the mammoth, record-breaking pumpkin in his niche. Paul specializes in making handmade high-performance leather sheaths for survival, tactical and hunting knives, which he sells online. His clients are survivalists, the folks who head off into the woods and stay there for weeks at a time with nothing but a knife (and a Hedgehog sheath). When they decide to walk back to civilization, they're wearing a suit they made out of tree bark and popping rattlesnake eyes into their mouths like they were gumballs. In other words, these guys are tough! They demand the best equipment and they surely don't use your dad's Swiss Army Knife. As an investor in Hedgehog for more than five years now, I have been able to learn a lot about the inner workings of this sheath-making giant.

Paul uses the Insider Strategy to great success. His clients win. His company wins. He wins. All because he genuinely wanted to connect with other outdoorsmen and survivalists in order to find out exactly what they wanted in new products. When Paul is getting ready to design a new sheath, he will reach out to the very tight-knit community of 10,000-plus subscribers via video, conference call or email and ask what they want. He'll say, "I'm getting ready to design a new sheath—which knife should I make it for?" He doesn't have to guess what he should make next. There is no focus group that could potentially march him down the wrong path, and he doesn't have to wonder if it will sell. Paul's entire community tells him exactly what they want, in effect, telling him exactly what they'll *buy*.

After Paul tallies up the responses, he makes sure he can work with the knife they've chosen, and then announces it to the community. "The majority of our community wants me to make a sheath for this knife, so here we go. I look forward to your feedback in the process."

Now, even the people who asked Paul to design a sheath for a different knife are interested in helping him develop this one because he clearly took their opinion into careful consideration. (It's like crack, I tell ya.) As he works on the design, Paul keeps the community engaged by sharing photos of his process: detailed videos and descriptive emails, sending out samples and hosting group conference calls for those who are invested in the outcome. And with the excitement of watching a product come to life, even if you weren't invested from the start, you get caught up in it along the way.

An added bonus—and really, the *reason why* Paul uses the Insider Strategy—is that he gets immediate feedback and great ideas and is able to harness the power of the "communal brain." He's collaborating with his clients, the end users, to create something unique, something he could not have created on his own. Paul has figured out the ultimate way of serving his best clients best, in real time.

When Paul is ready to sell the sheath, he makes it available first to the people who helped him develop it (and who can hardly wait to get their hands on it), and then only months, and maybe even a year later, to the general public. In following this process, Paul is able to predict how many sheaths he will sell to his community in the first month of the launch, with a very low margin of error. And his experience also helps him predict, with astonishing accuracy, how many he will sell to the general public. No kidding, he'll come within five or six units. Makes you think he has psychic superpowers.

And because his clients are collaborators, they promote the living hell out of these sheaths. They feel so connected to his products, to Paul, and to Hedgehog Leatherworks, they will talk all three up at the drop of a hat. They are Hedgehog diehards on a mission to convert other, unsuspecting survivalists to join their ranks. Sounds eerily similar to a cult, right? But what entrepreneur could ask for more than that?

THE SEQUENCE

When I launch a new product or service, I follow the same sequence every time. It's not that different than the launch process some of the more successful marketers follow—except for one, key difference: the predictor. I can say without any modesty that, when I follow this sequence to the letter, involving my community of clients and followers, it works every time. Every. Single. Time. And why shouldn't it? I'm giving the community exactly what they asked for, so why shouldn't they want it?

The sequence looks like this:

I. **Predict.** Ask your client base, your prospects, your followers and your fans if they would be interested in your new offering. Keep track of the number of responses (in relation to the total number of people in your database). Put way more weight on the responses from your top clients, rather than people who have loud voices. People who have bought in the past are likely to do so again. Get the conversation going by bringing out ideas from the Wish List.

2. **Appreciate.** Thank the people in your community who respond: the yes's, the no's and the maybe's. The fact that people care enough to respond is big. So you must show your gratitude. Even if they say, "This is the stupidest idea I've ever heard," email them and say, "Thank you so much for your honest feedback, it definitely helps give me direction."

3. **Announce.** If you're satisfied that you have enough "yes" responses to move forward, tell the community that since there are enough people who want your new offering, you're going to go ahead and create it. This will pique the interest of those who initially responded "no" because they'll naturally be curious about what the majority wants. It's like a standing ovation—you may not feel moved to stand up and clap at the end of the painful five-act

play that went on forever, but because everyone else is standing up, you get up and clap your heart out. It's human nature to allow yourself to be persuaded by the majority.

4. **Engage.** In any way you can, engage your community as you develop the new product or service. Keep them invested in the outcome by periodically giving them updates and asking their opinion. Let them participate as much as possible. Paul does this well. So does John Green, the *New York Times* bestselling young-adult novelist best known for his books *Looking for Alaska* and *Paper Towns*. He keeps his fans (dubbed nerdfighters) psyched about new books through his blog and videos, where he sometimes reads passages from his working manuscript. As soon as that book is available for pre-order, the nerdfighters come out in droves!

5. **Ask.** Request a small investment in the form of a deposit from people to get them committed to the process. Ask your community to put their money where their mouths are and they will be even more likely to follow through on the purchase. For example, Paul gets a $25 non-refundable deposit from those who say they want first dibs on a new sheath. He very matter-of-factly explains that it will help him figure out how many he will have to make before he purchases the raw materials. They get it, and they happily pay it.

6. **Limit.** When you launch your new product or service, make it available for a limited time and in limited quantities. And by all means, limit it to only the people who helped you bring it about. They will feel more special. And scarcity gets people moving. It makes purchasing your new offering—the one they helped create—a matter of urgency. Scarcity works. The fewer items

available and the less time there is to buy, the more likely people are to make a purchase. Threadless makes only a certain number of T-shirts. When the shirt is sold out, that's it, which is part of the reason why everyone wants to buy their new shirts . . . fast.

7. **Over-deliver.** One risk of using the Insider Strategy is that everyone is so involved in the process that they know exactly what they're about to get. They still want it—big time—but getting it is a little bit of a letdown. It's like me telling you every gift you're about to get the day *before* your birthday . . . bummer. So, the key is to deliver something more, or something unexpected. A surprise is a good thing.

8. **Keep Track.** Again, the beauty of the Insider Strategy over straight-up crowdsourcing is the predictability, but you can't predict anything if you're not measuring responses. Keep track of your data!

GUIDE THE SHIP

The Insider Strategy works so well, it will blow your mind. But remember, you still have to guide your business in the direction you want it to go. You can't let clients dictate every twist, turn and decision you make, as if your business is a *Choose Your Own Adventure* book and they're the one with all of the power, changing the outcome with every decision.

Clients only think about what they want. They don't think about overhead, resources, brand integrity or your long-range planning. You as the entrepreneur have to understand where a client wants to go, but if their demands can't be satisfied within your infrastructure—if they don't hit the sweet spot—you have to make the executive (that's you!) decision to let it go, or modify it to suit your business. John Green probably isn't taking plot advice from his nerdfighters, and if Paul Scheiter can't maintain his extraordinarily high quality sheath standard for a knife his community wants sheathed, he doesn't do it.

Recruit your clients to actively participate in building your next product or service in order to gauge interest and reduce risk. Encourage them to build sweat equity in your next offering, so that they have a higher degree of interest in buying it and are more likely to market it for you. Just remember—you're the captain of this ship. They are the wind beneath your wings . . . ahem . . . sails.

What if what customers want is too big? What if they want you to deliver a teleporter to them for five dollars, or something else that is impossible, given your capabilities? Tell your community you have reached an impasse. You can then take two courses of action. You could tell them the project they want won't be done in the near future and that you will start the runner-up project, or you could ask your crowd-sourced community to give you the solution. Schedule a call with your community to get their ideas. Get the handful of smartest and most committed people to give you guidance and direction. Who knows, maybe Spock is a hyped-up participant and gives you the blueprint for that teleporter after all.

Work the Plan—
Take Action in 30 Minutes (or Less)

I. *Schedule your sequence.* Before you dive in, schedule your sequence of steps so that if there is genuine interest for your big new idea, you have the time to respond to the interest, develop the product and launch it. You don't want to get people all hot and bothered over your new product or service idea and then leave 'em hanging.

2. *Test the waters.* Start with the predictor, the simple question that will help you gauge interest in your offering. Send it in an email, post it on your Facebook page, ask people on Twitter, ask clients when they come in to see you.

3. *Determine how you will engage and interact with your collaborators.* Will you make a video to share your progress? Will you post updates on your blog? Will you form a little group and meet every week to exchange ideas? Will you post updates daily on Twitter? Decide in advance so you're prepared to do the extra work to keep your collaborators engaged.

How to Pumpkin Plan Your Industry — Health Services

Let's pretend you own and operate a nursing home. Put down the meal tray, bypass the TV room and take a seat in your office. It's time to Pumpkin Plan your business.

Of all the nursing homes in a 100-mile radius, yours is the one that seems the most like home. The only problem is, you've got a lot of empty beds. Your competitors, with their big, slick, nondescript buildings have waiting lists a mile long, while you have an entire wing of empty rooms collecting dust. You try running an ad on television, which brings in, oh, about zero people. For some reason most of the elderly folks and their guardians are still choos-ing to sign up with your competitors.

So you identify your top clients: those people who rarely com-plain, always pay on time and have had more than one family member living at your facility. When you interview your top clients—residents and their families—to find out about their frus-trations with your industry, it comes as no surprise to learn that they don't like the commercial feeling of the big providers. They like the relaxed, casual atmosphere of your building. The "homey" décor, the way the staff treats everyone like family, the way the cafeteria doesn't seem (or taste) like a cafeteria at all, with its broad round tables and family-style meals.

But there is one "minor" issue: Your top clients are frustrated with the limited visiting hours and super-tiny parking lot. They wish that there was a way for them to stay more connected to their families (and vice versa) without having to wait for a visit. This aspect makes your place seem almost like a hospital.

And the tiny parking lot has many people forced to park about half a mile down the road next to a local coffee shop when they come for a visit. Many a family has canceled a planned trip to visit Granny and Grandpappy because they couldn't get into the lot. Not good. Not good at all.

So you talk it over with your team and brainstorm a solution to this problem. You present your ideas to your top clients to gauge their reaction, and modify your plan based on their input. You decide to bring in five new computers and hire a college student to help residents with email, Facebook and daily Skype sessions with their families. You recruit volunteers to sit down with residents and help them write letters to their families. You start videotaping events and posting them on Livestream and a secured YouTube channel—all while keeping your "home away from home" mission intact. Oh, and you make the no-brainer decision of extending visiting hours by an extra four hours every day. Yes, it costs more to staff. But, unhappy clients cost *a lot* more than that.

Next you tackle the parking issue. Due to environmental restrictions and zoning rules, you can't expand or modify the parking lot, so that's out. You can, however, reserve one parking spot at the building next door. So you buy a shuttle. Then, you meet with the coffee shop owner half a mile down the road (who happens to have a huge parking lot). You agree to install a dedicated courtesy phone in his shop, so when a family arrives they can go inside and call the shuttle. The coffee shop owner loves the idea, because now he has a family in his shop for five minutes until the shuttle arrives. And what do you think they do during those five minutes? . . . You got it, they order coffee (and sometimes pastries, because Granny loves chocolate-filled croissants).

All of your residents and their families love that you have made it easier for them to connect with each other. You can't help but notice that the residents smile more. They seem more relaxed. They laugh easily and talk to each other more often. A local news outlet writes a story about you that ends up in papers all over the region. You start to get calls from families looking to *move* their loved ones to your facility. You even get an inquiry from a woman who heard about your facility from a family waiting for the shuttle while in the coffee shop. Within a few months, your empty wing is full of new clients.

Then, you call your top clients and ask them if they would refer you to other vendors they use in relation to the care of their loved one. You get the names of several estate planners, health-care advocates and insurance agents. When you sit down with each of them and ask how you could help them serve their clients better, they are excited, and ask to learn more about your facility. You explain your mission, and share some of the changes you've made. Turns out, many of them are looking for a better way to communicate with residents and families at the same time, and you offer to let them set up Skype meetings with residents and families, using your Technology Coordinator (college kids love fancy titles).

Soon, you have happy residents, happy families and happy vendors who work with loads of other clients looking for nursing home facilities. These vendors refer people to you left and right. Within a year, investors approach you about building new, similar facilities in other parts of the state. Your reputation precedes you. See what a little problem solving can get you?

CHAPTER TEN

BIG, FAT & HEALTHY

Let's review how I became a Pumpkin Plan practitioner, shall we? My advisor Frank scared the crap out of me with the "one-nut guy" story, an article about giant pumpkins got me started, and then I applied the pumpkin-growin' strategies to growing my business. And just like a ginormous monster pumpkin, once I planted the roots for my business . . . it grew explosively.

After just two years, Olmec had earned seventy-five new *top* clients who were so aligned with my company, it was practically a mutual admiration society. How did I build my gigantor pumpkin? I did it through a process I like to call "tapping the vendor well."

This technique works so well that I think you are about to fall in love with me. Which in itself is bizarre, since the "me" is a book.

But I did hear a few years back about some Korean guy who married his pillow, ceremony and all. So perhaps it isn't out of the question . . . just be sure to send me (the author guy) the pictures from the wedding—you and the book all dressed up, exchanging vows, doing the funky chicken, feeding each other cake, honeymooning at some tropical island, taking hula lessons from Tom the Navy Seal.

But first, I need you to hold up for a sec. Before I tell you about this awesome technique, you must understand that this strategy does not work if you aren't already doing the things I've outlined in this book. The Pumpkin Plan is a step-by-step growing strategy, with each step building off the one before it. It's a progression—first you must have strong roots, then you must have constant vigilance on pulling the weeds, then you do this . . . watering like mad. So, if you haven't yet, please go back and do the work in Chapters One through Nine before you dive in to this one. If you don't, it just won't work.

Tapping the Vendor Well

I hit on this strategy back in my Olmec days, after I started working my own, more primitive version of the Pumpkin Plan. Things were better. Things were *good*, in fact. We had more money, less stress, better relationships with clients and zero rotten clients choking our progress. But while the one-nut guy no longer perched on my shoulder, mocking my every move, he still showed up in my dreams from time to time. I guess part of me still wondered if the proverbial other shoe (or other nut) would drop, and our decent business would once again become my own personal hell.

I looked at our client roster and noticed that hedge fund firms accounted for more than 30 percent of our annual revenue, yet we only had a few hedge fund clients, while the rest of our clients spanned a variety of industries. I remembered the 80/20 rule and realized we had to tighten our niche. We decided to label ourselves differently, and became Hedge Fund Technology Specialists. We changed our focus, message and branding to cater specifically to those clients. And, where we had once been the "computer repair guys" competing with hundreds of other "computer repair guys" in our own town, we now had two competitors . . . nationally.

The only problem was, I still hadn't figured out how to get *more* top clients. I knew they wouldn't just miraculously appear. And my prior door-knocking method took too much effort and had yielded almost no results. So that was out, too. Waiting for my top clients to refer me to other prospective top clients (which they did . . . sometimes) seemed like driving from L.A. to San Francisco by way of Michigan . . . on back roads . . . in a golf cart . . . with a wheel missing. It took *way* too long.

Then one day, I had an "aha" lightbulb moment. "If my top clients get me, and I get them, it stands to reason that they also have this relationship with other vendors who get them. And those vendors probably have a similar relationship with their own top clients. Just like I had my top ten favorite-est, best-est clients, these vendors probably had their top ten faves too. And, hot diggity, that vendor and I already had something in common . . . we both served one of my top clients. And because we had this in common, I could probably easily meet these vendors and ultimately I could share in their top clients."

Okay, maybe I wasn't that articulate, but I did have an instinct that my best clients' other vendors could be an untapped resource for new clients.

In the past, I had been a big believer in the "ask for referrals" protocol: Do a good job, and when you're done ask, "Are you happy with our work?" Wait for the yes. Wait for it. Wait . . . for . . . it. "Yes." Then, ask the cheesiest question ever invented in referral marketing: "Do you have any friends or contacts who would also benefit from our work?" Then watch the referrals pour in.

At least, that's how it was supposed to happen.

In my case (and I bet in yours, too) reality was way different. Asking clients for referrals brought uncomfortable moments for everyone involved, and instead of ending a project with a big "thanks," I was asking my client, who, mind you, was already paying me, to give me *more*. Awk-ward.

Put yourself in your client's shoes. You are asking them to do you a favor (after they already did you a *huge* favor by buying from you) and you are asking them potentially to put themselves at risk. If they refer you to someone else, you will be less available to them in the future. Or, you might share knowledge you gained on their dime with the new client. Or, you might not wow their friend, and now not only do you look bad, *they* look bad.

So, this half-baked way of asking for a referral often results in a halfhearted referral. In that uncomfortable moment, the client feels obligated to say yes, even though they don't want to. They may never refer anyone to you, or they may refer you to someone sucky, since they want you to stay their own little secret.

No more. I vowed to ditch the traditional "ask for referrals" process and create something new.

So I called Larry, my favorite of all my favorite hedge fund clients, and asked for a meeting. We met later that week and when I asked, "Besides me, which vendors are critical to your business and that you really like?" he said, "Why do you want to talk to them?" I expected that. It's not every day one of your vendors asks for referrals to *other* vendors. I noticed Larry's shoulders tensing up, as he pushed back from the table a bit. He was clearly uncomfortable.

"Larry, I want to give you the best possible service. To do that, I'd like to make sure I understand what your other key vendors do for you, and that any work I do for you integrates with and supports what they do for you. I want the work I do to give you the most bang for the buck by making sure that I don't put any roadblocks in the way of your other vendors," I explained. Larry seemed surprised . . . and impressed. Almost instantly his shoulders relaxed and he leaned in, smiling. Between you and me . . . the double Martini I ordered for him probably didn't hurt so much either.

"Oh. That's amazing!"

As Larry started ticking off names of other vendors he loved working with, I thought, "Wow, he is so much more relaxed than that time I asked him to refer me to other potential clients. Shoot, he's practically blurting out referrals."

Your clients don't want to risk referring you to someone else because they want to keep you for themselves. But this is different. Matching you up with other vendors in order to serve them better? *That* they can do. They *want* to do it. In fact, they think you're *awesome* for thinking of it, for caring about them so much that you would go out of your way to learn about their business and make sure everything runs as smoothly as possible. And if they didn't love your attempts to wow them with VIP service and wish lists, with under-promising and over-delivering, with finding new ways to make their lives easier and better and their business more profitable, they sure as shit *love* you now.

Finally, Larry handed me a piece of paper with a list of five vendors and the names of his main contact at each company. "Thanks. Which one do you depend on the most?" I ask.

Without hesitation he said, "Goldman Sachs." Goldman Sachs is the clearinghouse Larry's firm uses. All the money they move around gets the backing of Goldman, effectively becoming an insurance policy for Larry. This was, without a doubt, their key vendor.

"Do you mind if I talk with them and tell them what we talked about?" I asked.

"Sure." Again, no hesitation. Why? Because there's no threat.

Later that day I called up Ben, Larry's contact at Goldman Sachs, and asked for a meeting. I said, "Larry referred me to you. We're his Hedge Fund Technology Specialist, and I'm hoping we could meet so I can get your advice on how I should be working to make your job easier, and how we could both do a better job for Larry."

Did you notice how I asked Ben for advice? Catch that? "Asking for advice?" You're good. You're really good.

People (you included) love to share advice, it satisfies our egos. No one is above it. Me? Shoot, I wrote a book doling out advice. Can someone say, "major ego fix"?

Ben readily agreed to meet with me because he was flattered I would ask him for advice and because we already had something in common—a top client. When we met I briefly explained the work we did for Larry's company, and then I turned the conversation to be all about Ben and Goldman Sachs. I asked a lot of the same questions I ask customers when I'm trying to make their Wish List.

"What would make your job easier?"

"What do you wish Larry better understood about the work you do for him?"

"When would you like me to give you updates on what I'm doing with Larry?"

"What frustrates you about technology companies like mine?"

"What's your biggest gripe about working with hedge funds in this industry?"

Notice the last question is not specific to Larry. The last thing I want to do is diss our mutual client, and I don't want to make Ben (that is, Goldman Sachs) feel uncomfortable by selling him out. As I said in previous chapters, when you ask questions about an industry rather than about a specific person or business, you give people permission to share their complaints, concerns, ideas and secret wishes. It is like talking about the guy who has a booger hanging out of his nose—when he's not the room. No one dares say anything to his face, but the second he leaves, let the disgust-fest begin. We openly tell our true thoughts about a third party not privy to our conversations, and that's what you want. Feedback on the boogers of an anonymous thing like an industry.

Before we ended the meeting, I promised to get back to Ben soon with ideas about how we could work together to better serve Larry's company. And the best part was—this was not lip service. I was not trying to worm my way into Goldman Sachs' good graces by pretending to give a crap about wowing the pantaloons off Ben and his team. I really did want to wow the pantaloons off Ben and his team. (And yes . . . it was pantaloons, not pants—Goldman had this whole European contingent over there. Me personally? I'll stick with pants.) I'm in serious nurture mode here. I'm going beyond the normal care and feeding of hedge fund clients to grow the biggest, baddest pumpkin around.

And I'm excited. Genuinely excited. I live for this stuff, and it shows. Larry knows it. Pantaloon Ben knows it. Everyone knows it. And because Ben and his team could see how passionate and earnest I was about this, they trusted me—with their time, with their ideas and information, and with their referrals.

After I established a mutually beneficial relationship with Goldman Sachs, I asked Ben for another meeting. This time I told him, "I'd love to grow my business. Would you refer me to other clients who may need a Hedge Fund Technology Specialist? I would love to build on our working relationship with other clients, just like we did with our first."

What do you think Ben said?

Here's the thing: I'm not a competitor. And I'm *not* asking for referrals to his competitors. And I am *not* asking something of him that will dilute my availability to him. In fact, what I am asking will help him even more, and it will allow me to be *more* attentive to him. All I've ever done is help him out. I make him look good to Larry, our mutual client. Of course he's going to say yes.

"Absolutely," Ben replied, not at all hesitant. "Why don't you try this client?"

It's a small referral, a toe in the water. Ben wants to make sure I don't screw it up, but that's cool. I'm not worried. I'm rocking the Pumpkin Plan, so I *know* I'll rock this prospect's world. (Which I did.) And I also know that, because Larry and I get each other so well, and Larry and Ben get each other so well, that the new prospect and I will soon get each other very well, too. (Which we did.) *And* I know that when Ben notices how happy this new prospect is with my work, he'll send me one more referral, then another, and then another. (Which he did.) Let the waterfall begin.

One of the vendors Larry referred me to was Woodtronics, a company that made and installed the ergonomic trading desks that were a staple at hedge fund companies. Have you ever seen anyone work at a trading desk? It gets really intense. They curse, toss papers, curse some more, throw pens, curse some more, prowl around like caged animals, and curse at the fact that they curse so much—it's like a cage match, minus the fistfight. (Well, sometimes that happens, too.)

I had wanted to talk to the trading-desk guys for a while because, well, they kind of pissed me off. Every time they moved or added to the furniture, they yanked out our cables (not realizing what they were doing) plugging in their own cables, and then we'd yank out *their* cables (not knowing any better), and then the hedge fund guys would freak because the equipment they depended on—like *air*—broke down. Simply because I didn't get the other vendor and he didn't get me.

So we became friendly with the trading-desk guys. I asked, "How can I help you better serve Larry?"

"Stop yanking out our cables!"

"What? I was going to ask you not to yank *our* cables!" I said.

Which is when we realized what we'd been doing all along . . . we were yanking on each other's cable. (Cue the tasteless jokes.) So I said, "Well, could you show us how you'd like us to wire a trading desk properly?"

Yup. That's all it took. Once we learned how to service Larry's computers and not screw up the rest of the desk, the trading-desk guys loved us. The hedge fund guys loved us. Heck, we even loved *ourselves* more. (Cue more tasteless jokes.) Soon, without even asking, the trading-desk guys started referring clients to us left and right because they didn't want *any other* "cable yanker" servicing their clients (one more time for the tasteless jokes).

Holy . . . wow. Talk about an overnight sensation. Within months we had more prospects than we ever could have imagined. Sure, they weren't all worthy of top-client status, but we had our pick of clients. Who could complain about that?

Over the course of the next eighteen months Goldman Sachs

referred me to seventy-five of their top clients, who quickly became my new top clients. Seventy-five! I had figured out how to
tap the vendor well to expand my client base according to my new
Pumpkin Plan standards.

And with that, the one-nut guy disappeared from my dreams.
Didn't even leave behind any mementos of our time together. No
dentures fizzing away in a cup in my bathroom. No old-man smell
tickling my nose. He was gone . . . forever.

Move in Concentric Circles

When growing mammoth pumpkins, you don't spread your seeds
over seventeen acres; you focus on half an acre, plant one seed (or
two, if you're really ambitious) and focus on tending to and
strengthening that vine. Because you have limited resources (time,
marketing dollars, etc.) you can't be as effective or as visible if
you're covering too much territory.

When you focus on moving within one tight area, prospects
and clients see you more frequently. Once we tightened Olmec's
niche to working primarily with hedge fund companies, we started
hanging out where they hung out. We joined clubs, associations
and other groups to which they belonged. We advertised in their
trade publications. We went to lunch where they went to lunch.
We moved in concentric circles, focusing solely on hedge fund
companies until, in their eyes, we were ubiquitous.

There is a threshold of trust, a moment when you've seen someone enough times that you trust them. You think you know them,
even though you've never met. That guy from the fourth floor who

you run into at the coffee shop every morning—you don't know him, but because you see him every day, you start to think he's a "nice guy." He could be the biggest deviant on the planet, but because you've seen him enough times, you trust him. It works the same in business.

Market only to the locations where your key prospects are and they will believe you're everywhere. Show up at their industry conferences and trade shows. Attend their workshops. Buy a table at their fundraisers. Take a tour of their factories. Write a guest blog post for their online media outlets. They'll trust that you're the definitive expert, the go-to company for whatever products or services you offer. And, just like the coffee shop guy, after they begin to see you all the time, they'll naturally come to believe you must be a "nice guy."

When we re-branded Olmec from "the computer guys" to Hedge Fund Technology Specialists, we became, virtually overnight, one of three companies who specialized in servicing hedge fund companies. We no longer had to compete on price; we could compete on quality, or speed and efficiency. We could innovate and make a big splash, instead of a tiny ripple. We could cover this tight territory and just "be everywhere" to build trust with prospects and clients. We could team up with their other vendors to help our clients grow their businesses. We could form alliances with those vendors to refer other clients to each other, clients who could easily become contenders for top-client status.

With our tight niche focus, we could tap the vendor well, solve clients' problems (and take care of the stuff that really annoyed their vendors), move in concentric circles and develop a massive client roster of exactly the type of client we needed to grow into a multimillion-dollar giant of a company.

And it worked. Stick that in your corncob pipe and smoke it. Yes, a corncob pipe . . . that's how we farmers roll.

Work the Plan—
Take Action in 30 Minutes (or Less)

I. *Apply the 80/20 rule.* Look at your short list of top clients and determine which few clients (top 20 percent) bring in the most revenue (80 percent). In other words, in which industry do most of your high-revenue clients operate? Think about what you could do to re-brand your business with that tight focus. How could you better serve this niche industry? How many competitors would you have if you served this industry exclusively? With this tightened focus, how would you describe what you do?

2. *Tap the vendor well.* Call three of your top clients and request a meeting to find out about their trusted vendors. Prepare a list of questions in advance. Then, set up an appointment with at least one of the vendors that each client referred and team up to better serve your client. Eventually you're going to want to ask the vendor to refer you to their preferred clients, but for now, just help each other wow your mutual client.

3. *Start moving in concentric circles.* Now that you've tightened your niche, make a list of all of the places your prospects and clients are likely to appear, from online magazines to trade shows; from associations to charity events. Then, make a plan to show up to as many of these places as possible. Don't show up in "sell" mode; just be there.

How to Pumpkin Plan Your Industry — Professional Services

Let's pretend you're an attorney sitting in your office surrounded by leather-bound books and stacks of paperwork. Brush up on your E pluribus unum whompum shakira fandango and let's Pumpkin Plan your industry!

You have a healthy law practice, sharing space with a few other attorneys who, like you, are still paying off their student loans. You're making decent money, but you want to make *great* money. The problem is, you're too busy to even *think* about marketing, networking or even renewing your ad in the Yellow Pages.

After filling out the Assessment Chart, you decide to let go of the clients who take up so much of your time dickering over their bills that you have to stop yourself from addressing them as "Dick" when they call. (*That* was a no-brainer.) Then you axe the few clients who prefer shouting to talking, and focus on your top seven clients.

Lulu is the first client you call. You've never met Lulu—she lives two hours north and all of your business is conducted over the phone. You run through your list of interview questions, and when you get to "What frustrates you most about attorneys?" you're surprised to hear her say, "They won't read the contracts to me."

You've been reading the contracts to clients for years because you just want to make sure they *really* understand what's in there. This also saves *you* time and frustration, but you had no idea the clients appreciated it as much as Lulu seems to.

"Why is this important to you?"

"Because my audio reader is cumbersome, and I can't jump around in the contract, so it takes me forever to understand all of the finer points," she says.

"Audio reader? I don't follow . . ."

"You do know I'm blind, right?"

What? You've been working with this client for nearly a year and hadn't realized she's blind?

"Lulu, I had no idea."

"Wow. Well, that's amazing. I just assumed you read me the contracts because you knew I was blind. I thought I mentioned it when I hired you," she says, laughing. "Well, you inadvertently provided me with the best service any attorney has ever given me. Reading the contract with me over the phone is something I've come to depend on."

After you hang up with Lulu you look at your list of top clients and realize that Lulu referred you to Dawn, the wheelchair-bound disability activist, who referred you to Ramesh, the Deaf owner of a taco franchise, and you start to connect the dots. Without realizing it, you've become a go-to attorney for a handful of people with disabilities—all because you're just the kind of person who likes to read contracts out loud.

You think about the sign language interpreter you hired to help you communicate with Ramesh, and the handicapped-accessible ramps and bathrooms in the office you chose to rent. It's not like you gave it much thought at the time; it just seemed like the right thing to do. Turns out, you have a natural affinity for working with the disabled.

Now, you call up Dawn and Ramesh and ask how you could better serve them and their community. You ask, "How could I cultivate this?" You get a list of ideas from them, and from Lulu, and brainstorm some of your own. You come up with a plan for how to best serve the disabled community, and then run it by your top clients, tweaking it based on their feedback. When they start saying things like, "Oh, I have to tell Rebecca's team about this," and "Tom would leave his family attorney to get in on that," and "I should tell everyone about this at the next meeting," you know you're on to something—you know you've found your very own Atlantic Giant seed.

With your plan in place, you're ready to re-label yourself. No longer are you just another attorney in a sea of attorneys—now, you are the Disability Legal Strategist. You Google other "disability legal strategists" in your area and . . . wow, look at that! You're the only one. Hmm . . . I wonder who will get *all* of the disabled clients in search of legal services? You change all of your listings online, and in the dusty old Yellow Pages, to reflect your new label. *And*, because you have a new label, you can create your own pricing structure. You're not competing on price, or even convenience. You don't have to. You are in a league of your own.

You buy a TTY machine (for phone communication with Deaf clients) and take a sign language class to learn the basics. You re-design your office to better accommodate wheelchairs. You invest in Braille brochures about your services. Then, you start moving in concentric circles, showing up at local and regional conferences for people with disabilities, placing ads in related newsletters, speaking at disability support groups and volunteering for non-profits dedicated to helping people with disabilities. (You are *so* on it. Those student loans are going to be paid off in no time!)

Soon, you're working with hundreds of clients just like Lulu, Dawn and Ramesh—clients you are naturally suited to work with, clients who appreciate and respect you, clients who are so grateful to have an attorney who gets them and caters to them that they go out of their way to be the best clients ever.

Fast-forward a few years and your business is off the charts, the biggest pumpkin around, but you're ready to plant a new Atlantic Giant seed. It's time to grow another record-breaking pumpkin. So, playing off your existing root system, you launch a training company focused on helping attorneys, accountants and other professionals better serve the disabled community. You know *all about* how to do this, and now you're ready to build a business around that knowledge. And because you rocked the Pumpkin Plan the first time around, your next giant pumpkin is a sure thing.

CHAPTER ELEVEN

THE AIRLINE SAFETY CARD METHOD

After we landed seventy-five new clients in less than two years, my butt was dragging. Despite the fact that I had a team of technicians who could handle repairs, when certain clients called, I still left my desk, got in my car and drove out to their offices to personally handle the problem. Then, hours later, I'd head back into the office to catch up on *everything else* I had to do, which was, like, everything else that had to be done.

To make matters worse, there were constant distractions throughout the day, every day, from the very technicians I hired to reduce my distractions. They called me constantly with questions.

"Should I do this extra project the customer requested?"

"How do you do this or that procedure?"

"I just got an emergency call from customer B. Should I leave customer A to go handle it, or should I stay where I am?"

"Can I go on a lunch break?"

"Why is the sky blue?"

"Do you think I need a hair transplant?"

"Can you teach me how to play 'Stairway to Heaven' on my piccolo?"

As my company grew, I morphed into a stressed-out version of an adult babysitter. When I wasn't guiding my staff on their work, I was scrambling to do the work myself. My. Butt. Was. Dragging.

In my first business, I made the same mistake almost every entrepreneur makes: When my staff had too many questions, I would throw up my hands and just "take care of it" myself. I figured taking ten minutes of my own time would be better than taking ten hours to teach them how to do it right. I thought it would be easier if I just handled it, because the thought of having to train someone to take care of my important clients exactly the way I took care of them overwhelmed me. Quite frankly, I didn't actually *believe* anyone could take care of them as well as I could. (Hello, ego. You get me into so much trouble, dude.)

The stress of doing it myself was too much, so I went for the "instant fix." I reasoned that if I hired really experienced guys (and I mean tons of experience), I wouldn't need to teach them squat. They would just *know*. And if I was really lucky, then maybe, just maybe they would know better than me. Some of the guys I interviewed had twenty years of computer experience. These guys were so well versed, they had worked on computers back when there was a group of monkeys pedaling stationary bikes inside the car-sized machines, and all the computer could do was add stuff up slowly. You know, two plus two equals . . . wait for it . . . four.

I quickly discovered my mistake. Hiring experienced guys meant I was hiring years or decades of bad habits. While these technicians called me less often (they "knew" what they were doing after all), my clients were calling me *more* often . . . with complaints. The new "experienced" technicians were not following any form of protocol. They were undoing work we had previously done, changing settings and "fixing" things that didn't need to be fixed. Not because they were bad guys. Not because they were trying to do harm, but simply because the experienced guys "knew better" and did it their way. And their way caused huge problems.

You know that saying, "You can't teach an old dog new tricks"? Well, it's true. These experienced guys were not willing to learn one new thing from me. In their minds, they knew the best way, the only way. They had twenty years of experience, after all. So they rejected any direction I gave them. It ended up that the more experienced a technician was . . . the *more* problems I had. I had to spend more time fixing the changes he made. I had to spend more time mending the client relationship. Bottom line, I had to spend more time.

While I was shocked that my first fix didn't work, I had a backup plan that was sure to work. I figured that since the experienced guys hadn't worked out, and having a large team distracted me from getting any work done, it would be easiest and quickest to downsize to the "good old days." Instead of having a team of eight people that needed babysitting, I would go back to a team of one or two people. Me, one personal assistant and a grunt worker. My company was making good revenue at this point, and if I cut back to a support staff of just two entry-level employees, I could make killer money.

That plan fell apart when I realized the whole reason I had pushed to grow the company was because I was worn out from running a three-person company! Whether backed by a large team who needed constant attention or a small team who couldn't handle the workload, I was screwed. It was as if I had handcuffed my-self to the hamster wheel and thrown away the key.

Basically, I was stuck in a trap of my own making.

Perhaps you are in one of those traps right now. You can't find anyone who is as good as you, and you can't go back to the "good old days" because, let's be real: there were no good old days. We entrepreneurs just look back at those early days fondly because they *seem to have been* less complicated. We forget that we killed ourselves every day trying to run the show with little or no help.

I know it's hard to accept that you're stuck, but you're hardly alone in this one. It's super common. Most entrepreneurs struggle making the leap from a one- or two-person start-up to a business with ten or more employees. There are probably 8,097 reasons why we keep making this mistake over and over again, but the top offenders are scarily consistent: 1) we don't think we can afford to hire someone else to do it; 2) when we do hire someone with enough experience (and forgo our own salaries), they are unable or unwilling to do it the right way (our way); 3) even when we bring in someone we can afford, and who doesn't need to "un-learn" their experience, we don't have time to train them; and 4) even if we had the money to hire a willing and able staff and had the time to train them, we're fairly confident they would pale in comparison to our own superior abilities. (That last one? That's the biggie. I know you're awesome and I know you've had to do it all and be it all for a long time now, but you *can* let go. You have to. It will be okay. I promise.)

But there is a way. This book is about growing a giant, *significant* pumpkin, after all.

And you can't do that if you can't scale your business.

Here's your "come to Jesus" moment: You cannot scale your business if that means that you do most (or even some) of the work.

Period. In fact, if you want to grow a serious business, a Pumpkin Planned business, it requires that you don't do *any* of the work.

Remember in the Introduction when I said this book holds your key to entrepreneurial liberation? Well, this is exactly the "aha" moment you need to break free. If you're finally going to stop working *for* your business, and instead have your business *work for you*, you must ensure that not one ounce of your deliverable—not one thing that the client experiences—depends on your doing it. When you achieve this, your main job becomes building repeatable systems in order to ensure that every client has the same, the identical experience, every time.

Remember the sweet spot, the three components of finding your very own Atlantic Giant seed? The sweet spot is where your best clients, your unique offering and your ability to systematize intersect. Let's talk about that third and absolutely critical piece of the pie (pumpkin pie, in our case)—systematizing. This requires that you take a step back.

I know you love your business. Now it's time to love it more.

I know you're proud of the work you do. Now it's time to be proud of the work your company does.

I know you have mixed feelings about handing hard-won clients over to some newbie who just filled out his W4 form. But now it's time to have the confidence that a newbie can pull off the same quality work you would be doing yourself.

You get this. You know deep inside there's only so much of you to go around! Until you figure out the key to cloning yourself, you have to choose: either drag your exhausted butt all over town while you stunt your company's growth or finally build systems and train your staff to do the work for you (the thing you hired them to do) so you can grow, grow, grow. 'Cause it's their job . . . remember?

Become a Real Entrepreneur

Remember Frank, my business mentor? In Chapter One I told you how he burst my bubble (and bruised my ego) when he told me I wasn't really an entrepreneur, not yet. So you don't have to break your stride flippin' pages to find what I am talking about, here's what Frank said: "You're not an entrepreneur yet, Mike. Entrepreneurs don't do most of the work. Entrepreneurs identify the problems, discover the opportunities and then build processes to allow *other people* or other things to do the work and to do it right, consistently."

I still remember how awful it felt to hear that. Frank was basically telling me I was in a glorified job, trapped in that sell it–do it, sell it–do it, sell it–do it cycle that kept me running, broke and covered in red blotches. And here I thought I was my own man. In reality, my clients owned me just as much as my old dick of a boss had owned me.

The problem was, every time I sent someone else out to service "my" clients, I would inevitably get a call from one of them, complaining about mistakes, or that my guy "doesn't get our system," or asking, "Why can't you just come out, Mike?" In an effort to keep our clients, I kept pinch-hitting, taking precious time away from *growing* my business to *work in* my business. My staff wasn't *that* bad. They got things right 99 percent of the time. They did everything they were supposed to do, but they just forgot to say hello to the contact when they arrived or forgot to turn off the lights when they left. That one percent wrong bothered my clients enough that they were upset. And that was a real problem.

Then I remembered what Frank said about "building processes," and I asked myself a better question: "How could I systematize servicing this client so that anyone on my staff could do it and my client wouldn't know the difference between them and me?" Bingo! That was the right question, because soon enough I was doing one of the things I do best—designing systems.

Don't get me wrong; it wasn't a quick-and-dirty brain dump. Designing a system so thorough and easy to implement that anyone on my staff could follow it and pull it off perfectly was a long, involved process. But in the end, I was able to let go of the "doing" *and* keep my clients happy. In the end, I was an entrepreneur.

Building a system did take ten hours, when I could have just done it myself in ten minutes. But when I ran the numbers, I realized that I had had to do it myself for ten minutes about twenty times a week. That meant that within just three weeks, I'd have used up those ten hours, with no end in sight.

This is when I had one of the biggest "duh" moments of my life. Building systems is simply another form of investment. I had invested in my business with cash to start (about $100, which was some really big money at the time). The next investment was sweat—mine. For years I toiled away at servicing the clients. But this investment was no longer a possibility. I couldn't work any more hours or any more days. It was just physically impossible. This is when I realized taking the time to build systems and constantly improve upon them so that others could execute the systems with perfect consistency was simply a new investment strategy. And just like any other investment, the immediate return was minimal; but over the long term it was *huge*.

A system done right is a masterpiece, an example of perfect simplicity. Now don't get me wrong, systems do not simplify the results; systems simplify the process of getting there. Maybe a little lesson in flying would help . . .

Break it down

When was the last time you actually looked at the airline safety card stuffed into the seat pocket in front of you? I'm guessing the last time you looked at it was on your first flight. And you probably don't even watch the little flight-attendant show before takeoff, anymore (unless there is a cutie up there).

The next time you fly, pull that laminated sucker out and take a good look at it. It's an amazing example of a beautifully designed system anyone can follow. It's practically a work of art. No, really. I'm totally serious. Think about it—the airline safety card has to be easily understood by *everyone*. Grown-ups and kids, people with special needs, people who don't speak English, people who can't *read*, people who watch too much reality TV, people who live in a bunker and never watch *any* TV . . . anyone and everyone.

And knowing what is on the card is not enough! You or the seven-year-old to your left (who just spilled juice in your lap) or the 107-year-old to your right (who just "spilled" drool in your lap) may actually have to execute the darn thing. If something goes haywire, one or all of you may have to act fast and help lots of people safely exit a very dangerous situation.

Guess what? Everyone gets it (even the seven-year-old) and everyone can do it (including Grandpa Droolfest). Including you. Including me.

When I design systems for my businesses, I always follow what I have dubbed the "Airline Safety Card Method"—I break it down, and break it down, and break it down until the system not only fits on one laminated sheet, but becomes easy for anyone to understand and implement. Then, I take it for a test drive. If my receptionist can do it, if my sales staff can do it, if the pizza delivery guy can do it, it's ready for prime time. If not, I go back to the drawing board and keep at it until they can.

Let me be clear about one thing: this can be excruciatingly tedious. Even if you had all the time in the world, you would grow tired of taking apart your methodology, the work that at this point is probably second nature to you. It can be hard to explain. You just "do what you do," right? It's your own thing. No one can duplicate it.

Wrong.

Anyone can duplicate it . . . if you take the time to show them how. Your systems can only be mastered when they can fit on your own version of the Airline Safety Card. The process seems so easy. Just look out the window to make sure it is safe, pull the red handle to open the door, pull the yellow tab, and the safety slide shoots out. Then jump onto the slide and pull the tabs on your life vest, blowing into it if it fails to inflate.

For the airline passenger (employee) the process is incredibly simple. But for the airline industry that developed it, it required decades of effort. Just think about the slides. They stay tucked inside the airplane and during an emergency, pop out fully inflated when a single tab is pulled. Then, with fifty people hanging on for dear life, the slides turn into a raft that can float away and navigate ocean waves with the pull of yet another single tab—that's hard core. The system is amazing. It saves lives. Decades of work on a system allows people to work the process easily, simply and quickly. When you put the effort into developing systems in your business, the rewards can be just as big.

Imagine how fast you could grow your business if you could count on your team to deliver superior service or turn out quality products every time. What projects could you say yes to that you turned down in the past? In what areas could you expand your business that you couldn't before? How many top clients could you take on and nurture? And the ultimate question . . . Could you finally go on vacation, and be making money while you are away . . . for an entire month?

See how the Airline Safety Card Method frees you up?

THE THREE QUESTIONS

If you are like many of the entrepreneurs I have worked with face to face, I bet I know exactly what you are thinking right now. Just don't get weirded out. "OK, Mr. My-cow-shits"—another of my favorite nicknames from high school—"my business is way more complex than an airplane crash landing. I mean a plane crashes into two things, the ground or the water. While it is a serious situation, it is predictable. My business is unpredictable. I can run into hundreds, nay, millions of different situations. How do I teach my team to handle that?" (I hope I didn't freak you out by predicting your thought would include the word "nay." I am just that good.)

You empower your team to handle unpredictable situations by employing the Three Questions. As you build systems, you also give your staff direction on how to manage their thoughts. No, I'm not talking about Big Brother thought control. I'm just saying you have to develop systems that will help your staff *think* like you and, as a consequence, act appropriately in unexpected circumstances. When you develop systems to execute the work the way you do and the systems to think the way you do, well, I guess you've done the impossible—you've kinda cloned yourself. Better yet, you've built a business that doesn't need you toiling away in it for another single day.

Over the years I've developed Three Questions, three simple but darn powerful questions that, when asked in a particular sequence, allow employees to think and to reach decisions that are always in the best interest of your company. These questions are so effective, you may want to print them out on a piece of paper and paste it above each employee's desk . . . or tattoo it to everyone's forehead. Scratch that one. They wouldn't be able to see it.

Here are the Three Questions, in order:

1. Does this decision better serve our top clients?

2. Does this decision improve or maintain our Area of Innovation?

3. Does this decision grow or maintain our profitability?

Before your employees make a decision or take action, they must first ask themselves these Three Questions. If they can't answer with a definite "yes" for each question, they know not to proceed. Heck, *you* should be asking yourself these questions every time you have to make a decision. Should you develop that product, cancel that service, change locations, take on a new partner, switch vendors, change your prices? I don't know—did you get three yeses?

You know by now that the key to Pumpkin Planning your business is to be manically focused on your top clients. The client is the be-all and end-all. Everything you have done to this point is to better serve your top clients. Well, guess what? Your employees need to take up that quest . . . always improving the experience of the top clients. Your staff must always think of the top clients first.

To go to the next question, an employee must definitely have said yes to the one before it. Once they are confident that the top clients will be better served by their decision, they need to ensure that it is also in the best interest of your client/company relationship. The Area of Innovation is what distinguishes you from the competition and is the main reason clients buy from you. Always push the envelope with respect to your AOI, and it will keep you in front of your competitors. By embedding it in the system of thinking for your employees, you will automatically push the AOI forward. Win for you. Win for the clients.

Finally, you need to make sure you are making money. If an employee says no to the third question, they have started you down a dangerous path. Even when you have happy clients and cool innovations, losing money still leads to bankruptcy. Too many companies slowly chip away at their profit because, hey, two out of three ain't bad, right? Wrong. In the end, they're scrambling to save their company from financial disaster.

Yes to all Three Questions means go. Employees can just do it, no need to consult with you. No need for you to give them any blessing. No magic wand. Just go. If they can't say yes to all three, the answer is just as clear. Stop. Don't do it.

Now, when you look at these questions, you have to do something you may have not done in the past . . . you have to teach your employees who the top clients are, and why they are top clients. You have to teach them what makes you special (AOI) and what they can do to make your company even special-er. And you have to teach them how your business makes money and pays for things—like, their salaries. In other words, you need to give them a sense of ownership in the outcome. And this, as Martha says, is a good thing.

Enforcing the Three Questions system is pretty simple; it just requires stick-to-itiveness. The next time an employee asks you how they should proceed in a given situation, ask them to walk you through their internal discussion on the Three Questions. (Hint: If they are asking you for direction, it is unlikely they actually asked themselves the Three Questions.)

Will the Three Questions work for everything in your business? No, they won't. Next time you order toilet paper, it is unlikely it will better serve clients (unless they like to sneak over to use your john), and it probably won't make your profits grow. But when it comes to client services and products that clients consume, these three questions have yet to fail me.

Once you've shifted out of the do-it-all-yourself mentality, you'll be building systems efficient enough to fit on your own version of the Airline Safety Card. You and your people will be empowered with the Three Questions you need to determine if you're making the right move in any given situation. Congratulations. You're an entrepreneur.

Work the Plan—
Take Action in 30 Minutes (or Less)

I. *Break it down.* Take the task you perform most for clients and break down how you do what you do. Whether you're providing a service or manufacturing a product, detail the process from start to finish. What are the key components? What are the little tricks or quirks you employ that really impress your clients? What are the absolute no-no's? Jot it all down, even if at this point it seems like you'd need a billboard on which to fit all of the information.

2. *Break it down again.* Now go in and fill in everything you missed. Because you did forget stuff. What are the key steps you follow that you just do automatically? What do you do differently

than your staff? Why do your clients prefer to work with you? What are your clients' silent expectations? How do you under-promise and over-deliver?

3. *Break it down one more time.* Next, take everything you've downloaded about how you do what you do and condense it into easy-to-follow steps. You're not writing a manual here; you want your very own Airline Safety Card version of this system.

4. *Print it!* Print out the Three Questions and hang it above your desk. Get in the habit of always asking the Three Questions when you face decisions. New website? Ending a service? Hiring a new employee? Run each decision through the Three Questions filter. Then once you have a feel for this system, print it for everyone, put it above their desks and start practicing.

How to Pumpkin Plan Your Industry — Hospitality

Let's pretend your lifelong dream is to open a restaurant. You have always been known among family and friends for your culinary artistry. This is your chance to show the world. Put on that apron and pour yourself a drink. This is one way to Pumpkin Plan your industry.

You run a restaurant that specializes in gourmet comfort food, the stuff your grandma used to make. You thought you'd be pack-ing 'em in, every table booked with people dying for Granny's Goulash. But instead, you're competing with ten other restaurants in a two-block radius ... and not very well. Even though you almost always have empty tables, you're working 19-hour days and borrowing money from your mom to advertise in the local Pennysaver.

You start with your Assessment Chart, basing it on the twenty customers you see most often. The Andersons, Blaine and Charlotte, come in three nights a week with their five kids—they're so obnoxious, your waitstaff plays rock-paper-scissors to see who has to serve them (and one of the staff used real scissors just to *make sure* he doesn't end up with the Andersons). Bill and Steve, the lawyers, bring in clients for lunch nearly every weekday, dropping more on booze than they do on food. And of course there's Mrs. Trumpet, the sweet old lady who shows up every Tuesday and Friday at four-thirty for an early-bird discount (you don't have one) and always sends her food back three times. Filling out your list are the three theater couples, the six entrepreneurs who frequently bring in prospects, and a handful of couples who come out every Saturday for date night.

After you fill out the Assessment Chart, you know which customers make your life hell (hello, Andersons) and cost you money (talkin' to you, Trumpet), so you cut them loose. Since it's against the law to deny someone service just because you don't like them, you've got to figure out what would make them want to stop coming to your restaurant.

You've had enough of broken glass, crayoned walls and noisy kids, and you've figured out that it's not just the Andersons who have to go—it's all families with kids. It's not that families with kids are a bad thing (you have two kids yourself, after all), it's that families with kids are scaring away the big-money clients who want your restaurant to be a mini-vacation—delicious food coupled with sophisticated conversation.

Since you usually don't have much business before 8:00 p.m., you change your hours, opening for dinner at 7:00 instead of 5:00, well after parents are giving their precious bundles a bath. (Sneaky, but effective.) You get rid of the kids' menu and ban strollers from the restaurant. (Bold. Very bold.) Sure you're going to catch hell on the mommy blogs and forums, but you don't want them there anyway, right? The Andersons are pissed, but they get over it, and move on to bug your main competition, two doors down.

And because you changed your hours, Mrs. Trumpet hates you. She'll "never eat in your establishment again." Touchdown! Your waitstaff is so happy, they buy you one of those cheesy "#1 Boss" mugs, high-five you a lot and vow not to use real scissors for rock-paper-scissors ever again.

You look at all expenses related to serving families. You stop ordering frozen chicken fingers and fries, eliminate your crayon budget, watch your linen cleaning bill plummet, and stop running ads in the local parenting rag. (Now that you're not borrowing money from her to pay for the ads, Mom loves you, too.) Since you no longer have to make room for strollers or high chairs, you add a few more tables to bring in more revenue. Nice.

Now that you've eliminated the group that bugs you the most and pays you the least, you can focus on your top clients. You decide that Bill and Steve are the best clients ever, and the entrepreneurs are a close second. So you decide to focus on professionals entertaining clients. The next time Bill and Steve come in, you go up to their table and ask if you could sit with them for ten minutes. (Your mission: get their Wish List.)

You ask, "What do you wish all restaurants would do for you? How can we make your experience here perfect?" You give them a few ideas to get them comfortable with the idea that they *can* ask. "For example, would you like the ability to set up an account, or make special requests for wine or food?" You get their pet peeves about your industry. "What frustrates you most about restaurants?"

And this is where the big, shocking, totally unexpected discovery is made. Bill and Steve point out that a lot of business discussions and sales go down in your restaurant. They prefer to meet clients at your restaurant because the food is great and the location is ideal. They tell you that when they're eating in your restaurant, they are almost always on the clock. The problem is, their clients frequently step away to answer their cell phones, and when they do, Bill and Steve are off the clock.

This is when they let you in on their big wish: could you make the restaurant a cell-phone-free zone? You tell them it's a great idea, you'll put up a sign the next day, and of course you get right on over-delivering on that promise. When Bill and Steve come in again, they notice the "No Cell Phones" sign on the door, and smile. They're happy. You listened. You care. You want to help them put money in their pockets.

But you've also come up with a genius idea. You tell Bill and Steve that you've installed a device that jams cell-phone signals, so that even if clients disregard the "No Cell Phones" sign, they still won't get calls at the table. Genius! Bill and Steve are thoroughly impressed—after all, you just boosted their billable time, big-time. You went above and beyond for them; they are your customers for life.

You know asking for client referrals is not often fruitful. So next, you ask for vendor referrals to other hospitality providers Bill and Steve love to use. One of the referrals you get is for a limousine company, Bob's Elite Car Service. You call Bob and ask him for a meeting to brainstorm ways you can help serve your mutual clients better.

Bob mentions that he has a car drop off a client at your place at least once a week. You had no idea. You start asking any and every question on how to make his job easier.

"Do you need a special parking spot? Do your drivers need a heads-up from one of our servers when Bill and Steve are about to pay the check, so your drivers can 'magically' show up just as the client walks out the door? Would you like a little table in the kitchen so your drivers can grab a bite while they're waiting? Would it help if we had a to-go cup of coffee or bottle of water for them?"

Bob has been in the business for more than twenty-five years now, and he has never had anyone offer to help in the way you are. Not even close.

Now you and Bob are best friends, so Bob tells all of his drivers to recommend your restaurant to their high-profile clients looking for a restaurant. Suddenly you're packed with men and women in suits, ringing up big checks while they wine and dine clients over Grandma's Goulash. See how that works?

CHAPTER TWELVE

KILL THE CURVE

The morning after I sold my share of Olmec I started a new business. (No rest for the obsessed, am I right?) I'll admit it . . . I'm a junkie. Once I figured out how to engineer explosive growth for my first business, I was hooked. I could have taken a few months off to just chill, but once you know how to raise a fast-growing, successful business from one tiny seed of an idea, you kind of want to do it over and over again. If you've been implementing all you've learned in this book, you'll see what I mean soon enough!

With a new business partner, I formed a computer forensics company . . . kind of like *CSI*, but with less blood. I didn't put a penny into it, and in the first year we grossed $600,000; in the second year, $1.7 million and in the third year, just before I sold my share of the business, we already grossed $2.5 million and were on a run to do $7.25 million the following year.

Most of our early clients were private businesses looking for evidence of wrongdoing within their own companies, or individuals looking for proof to support their claims in court. However, within six months of launching, I noticed we started getting calls from attorneys who were looking for someone, *anyone*, who would take their clients on. Most computer forensics companies were run by former law-enforcement people, who, as it turned out, wouldn't touch criminal-defense cases. Attorneys literally could not get a forensics company to help them.

I thought, "Do I want to deal with defense attorneys trying to get murderers, embezzlers and white-collar criminals off?" I realized that these people *could* be innocent, and even if they weren't, we could find the evidence to prove it either way. We were simply purveyors of the truth. We found evidence and produced it. Guilty or innocent, admitting or denying, the evidence always spoke the truth. (See? Totally *CSI*.)

So, overnight we became one of the very few (if not the only) forensics companies willing to take on clients for criminal-defense attorneys. Despite my best efforts, I couldn't find a single competitor . . . and neither could our clients. This is how we made a name for ourselves almost overnight. We didn't have to pound the pavement or invest buckets of cash to market our business. Clients came to us in droves and we could take our pick. It was a beautiful thing. Beautiful.

In our second year, Enron called. (Yes, *that* Enron.) They were embroiled in the Nigerian Barge trial, and it was the beginning of the end. Kenneth Lay and crew needed forensics for their criminal defense, and by now we had the reputation. We were the obvious choice. We were the *only* choice. We took it, and after six months our team of three people found what the government could not find—proof that Enron was in cahoots with Merrill Lynch to screw with the financials and inflate profits. It's a long story—you can Google it. Let's just call them lying liarsons and be done with it.

As soon as my team found the trail of evidence no one else could find, Enron's attorneys had my guys on a private jet in thirteen minutes—they didn't want my team to be deposed by opposing counsel. Ultimately, it didn't matter, because they all went to jail. But it was official—we were the best of the best.

Which is how we landed even more clients, even some celebrities (though I won't name names).

By focusing on serving clients who were under criminal investigation, we took ourselves out of the running for other types of investigations, which meant we were no longer vying for a position in that marketplace. Instead, we started our *own* marketplace, where we were the only option. Sure, competitors popped up, but they were just pale imitations. And, because we rocked our niche, soon we landed other, non-criminal clients. It just happened. I worked the Pumpkin Plan *for sure*, but a key factor in our success was, we didn't just kill off diseased clients, we killed the curve.

What curve?

You know what sucks about the bell curve? You're graded based on how well everyone else does. So if you're not a genius, and you want to ace a test, you've got to pray half your class has a hangover or forgot to study.

The product-to-market curve looks just like the bell curve, except everyone is trying to find the best place to land on the curve so they can dominate the market. They want to get in on the market early enough to make the most of "consumer demand." People wrongly assume that the curve represents consumer demand, but in actuality, it represents the demand *based on the supply.* In other words, it's not what people want; it's what their best option is among the things that are available. And it's not that consumer demand wanes over time; consumer demand shifts based on what is available. Consumers don't get tired of products or services; they respond to innovation.

So let's talk VCRs. (If you're under the age of twenty-five, VCRs were magical boxes that played movies on large cassette tapes. Hold it. You don't know what a cassette tape is, either. Whatever. Anyway, you could now watch movies at home—yes, there was a time when you had to go to an actual movie theater to watch a movie . . . unless it was on TV . . . okay, moving on.) Not surprisingly, Americans went crazy for VCRs because, for the first time ever, they could watch movies at home, and manufacturers went crazy trying to get in on the action. It was a competitive market, until the DVD player came out, and suddenly you could watch movies with extras on DVDs that never wore out. DVD players wounded the VCR curve, for sure, but didn't kill it completely because it was still a variation on the same product. And while DVDs could play movies better than VCRs, VCRs could record television better than DVDs.

But then TiVo came out and, holy hell, people *flipped.* Now they could record their favorite television shows without having to take a class in programming their VCR, they could record multiple shows and even *pause* the television. TiVo didn't just kill the VCR curve, it annihilated it.

Entrepreneurs screw up when they try to get in early on the curve and work their way to the top of the heap. They see a trend and they want in on it. The problem is, now they're focused on outplaying the competition, when they should be focused on playing an entirely different game than the competition.

You know you're on the curve if you can say, "I have competitors." When you evaluate and judge your performance against your competitors, innovation is lost; you're just trying to build a better VCR. And at my last garage sale, I couldn't unload my old beast for a measly five dollars.

You've got to stop worrying about where you are on the product-to-market curve. You've got to create something so radical, it makes the curve obsolete. You've got to kill the curve.

THE 180 TECHNIQUE

In Chapter Eight I talked about how, if you label yourself in the same way your competitors label themselves, customers won't be able to distinguish how you are different. It's too complex for them. They can't sort it out, and they don't even want to try.

One way you can kill the curve is by giving yourself a new label. Cirque de Soleil did it. Rather than compete with all of the circuses of the world, they decided to label themselves differently. They became Cirque de Soleil. The new label hints at "circus" but at first glance it is different, and therefore begs prospective customers to ask, "What does that mean?" The grand opening provided by a unique label.

But Cirque de Soleil went much further. They changed the circus experience completely by pulling a 180. They completely changed how circuses deliver the entertainment experience (think rock music and lots and lots of acrobats, with tights that are way too, well, tight). They were not a different kind of circus; they created something else entirely, something new. They created their own curve.

When you're starting a new business, or rebuilding what you already have, give your business the new label first. Because your clients can't easily quantify the new label, they will say, "What does that mean?" That is your doorway to begin explaining how you are different, the components of your business or offering that make up your 180.

A label, after all, is just a name. You need to back it with some real street cred. You need the goods. You do that with the "180 Technique," one of my favorite ways to kill the curve. First you do an analysis of your industry and define all of the parameters— what are all of the assumptions about how this industry runs? Then, you ask yourself, "What is the exact opposite of that?"

For example, consumers understand three things about gas stations: they are outside, smell like gasoline, and if there is an attendant, he or she says three words to you (at most). The exact opposite of that would be an indoor, odor-free, climate-controlled gas station complete with a concierge who fills your tank, checks your oil, washes your car and makes your dinner reservations. (I still haven't worked out how you get rid of the gasoline smell indoors. Thinking some kind of air filtration, vacuum thingy. But, you see where I'm going with this.)

Commerce Bank (now TD Bank, N.A.) pulled a 180 with its "No Stupid Fees, No Stupid Hours" campaign. Commerce Bank stopped taking cues from other banks and started behaving more like a fast-food restaurant. Suddenly customers could bank when it was convenient for them, and they weren't penalized for every little error. Suddenly customers could get same-day service for things that other banks took days to handle. And suddenly, Commerce Bank didn't look like just another bank anymore. They had killed the curve. At a time when many banks were struggling, Commerce Bank just kept growing, and growing, and growing.

Look at video-rental stores. It used to be that you went to your local video store to pick up the latest movie on VHS. You would go in, look through the hundreds of movies lined up like books on a shelf, and try to find the newest *Lethal Weapon*. But because the store only had one measly copy, and someone rented it six years ago but never returned it, you wound up watching *Terms of Endearment* . . . again.

Blockbuster arrived on the scene and pulled a 180, giving customers access to dozens, sometimes more than one hundred, copies of new releases—you could rent the latest movie even if you walked in just before closing. They also displayed them differently, facing them out so people could easily spot the movie they were looking for. Blockbuster killed the curve so thoroughly, almost all of the independent video stores went out of business. Hollywood Video and other chains followed the curve, becoming copycats, and competed with Blockbuster for market share, but could not beat them. Why? Because Blockbuster created the curve and continued to push the curve to new levels—the others were just fighting over scraps.

Enter Netflix. They did the exact opposite of Blockbuster: instead of a per-movie rental charge, they charge one monthly fee; instead of going to the store to pick out a movie, your movie arrives at your house in the mail; instead of crazy late fees, you can keep the movie for as long as you want, with no penalties. Netflix pulled a 180 on Blockbuster, effectively killing the curve yet again. By 2010, Blockbuster had filed for Chapter 11 bankruptcy protection.

And the curve Netflix created? Some other company will come in and kill it. Maybe it will be Redbox or Roku. Maybe it will be something that defies our imagination. The only thing we know for sure is, it's coming . . . and it will be a radical departure from Netflix.

Notice that Commerce Bank, Blockbuster and Netflix all pulled 180s that addressed the chief consumer complaints in their industry. Crappy hours, slow service and high fees were the norm in banking—which annoyed the hell out of me, you and every other red-blooded American. The mom-and-pop video rental store was a constant source of disappointment because they only had one freakin' copy of the movie you wanted to watch! And though Blockbuster solved that problem, the complaints about their late fees were legendary—so legendary that people joked about it on TV, in movies, in our popular culture.

If you want to create a new curve, you've got to do the crazy thing, the thing no one expects. And that crazy thing you do? It should be genuine. Don't pull a 180 just to show off. Do it because it will solve something on your clients' Wish List. Do it because you want to defy the status quo in the best interests of your client base. Do it because, when you create a new curve . . . you own it.

Put an "est" on It

Another way you can create a new curve is to put an "est" on what you already do. Be the fastest, the cheapest, the slowest, the sexiest, the funniest, the scariest, the cheesiest, the strangest, the coolest, the coldest—be the "est." Everyone knows about the

ICEHOTEL in Sweden, but no one knows about the hundreds of thousands of hotels that just have bad air conditioning!

If there was a *Guinness Book of World Records* for your industry, you want to be in that mother, smiling like the goofball you are. There's no competing with the "est," so get on that. You'll create your own curve in no time.

Work the Plan—
Take Action in 30 Minutes (or Less)

1. *Analyze your industry norms . . . and then do the opposite.* What behaviors, systems and policies are considered "normal"—or even mandatory—in your industry? Analyze the parameters and identify the common spoken or unspoken rules of your industry and then figure out how you could flip them to create something totally new and unexpected. Remember, if you pull a 180 it has to be genuine and it has to fit within your sweet spot. Otherwise, you're just showing off for the cameras.

2. *Go back to the Wish List.* Oftentimes the 180 strategy is used most successfully when it solves a problem clients routinely complain about. Go back to your clients' Wish Lists and look for complaints you could address that would really turn your industry on its head and allow you to create a new curve.

3. *Find your "EST."* When you're the "est" of something—the biggest, the brightest, the smelliest—you can create your own curve. To find your "est," go back to your Area of Innovation (AOI), which we talked about in Chapter Two, and take it from there. If your

AOI is price, then obviously you need to be the cheapest date around. If it's speed and efficiency, you could be the fastest (duh), but you could also be the easiest, or the readiest, or the handiest. If your AOI is quality, then you've got a lot of "est" to play with. You could be the prettiest, the boldest, the happiest, the smartest . . . oh wait, this is starting to sound like high school. Then again, maybe that's not so weird, because when you find your "est" you quickly become "most likely to succeed." What? Too corny for you? Don't shoot me. It was right there . . . I had to do it.

CHAPTER THIRTEEN

NEXT SEASON

Before I sold my share of my first business, I knew I would start a new business. I had a plan. Before I sold my share of my second business, I knew I would start Obsidian Launch, my third business. I'm growing Obsidian Launch right now, just like you're growing your business. I will eventually sell it—I'm thinking in about, oh, ten years, give or take a couple (or perhaps when a golden opportunity presents itself), and I'll probably start yet another new business . . . maybe even the very next day. Regardless, I'll have a new idea, a new Atlantic Giant seed, before I sell. In fact, I am going through my options now. Slowly. Selectively. Deliberately. I am not rushing my next Atlantic Giant seed. I'm growing a giant pumpkin right now, so I'm not in a rush. But when planting season comes around again, I'll be ready.

Why do I do this?

Well, it's partly because I'm obsessed with launching and growing big, fat, successful businesses. (My wife would argue that it's also partly because I'm a little nutso . . . obsessed/nutso, toe-may-toe/toe-mah-toe.)

And it's partly just because there's a season for everything . . . even businesses. Pumpkins don't last forever. Eventually you're going to have to plant a new seed and start all over again.

The Pumpkin Plan works in part because of a laser focus on top clients, to the point where you're building an entire niche product or service around their needs. But that means that if that industry dies, your business dies. If all hedge fund companies had gone up in smoke, my first company would have followed shortly thereafter.

Pumpkins die—even giant pumpkins. This is why you need to extract a seed from that giant pumpkin of yours and use it to plant a new one . . . when you're ready. Do this *only* when your first pumpkin is rock-solid strong and operating on autopilot. Do I need to remind you of the farmer scrambling to keep all the pumpkins growing simultaneously? It is exhausting and fruitless (ahem . . . vegetableless). One giant pumpkin at a time; then, when it is big, strong and healthy, get the next one planted.

How big is big? For some businesses, big is the $10 million mark; but it could be $100 million or even $1 billion. Regardless, I have never seen it happen for companies with gross revenue of less than $10 million (but I'm sure it can happen).

Don't freak out. I'm not telling you to sell your business and start a new one. I'm telling you to prepare to grow something new. Maybe you'll evolve your business—that's what IBM did, leaving computer manufacturing behind to grow a new service business. You may find a new niche that allows you to both exploit your number-one strength and better serve your top clients (think of countless came-out-of-nowhere start-ups like Crocs or Google); maybe you'll start a new curve; TiVo did this by busting the VHS industry curve. Or maybe you *will* sell your giant pumpkin and start a new business. But it's inevitable. In order to stay in the game, you're going to have to grow *something* new.

Super-successful entrepreneurs know how to reinvent themselves and reinvigorate their companies. In the introduction to this book I talked about the legend that is the late Steve Jobs. He's a perfect example of a Pumpkin Planner who kept planting the seeds of remarkable businesses. First he launched Apple, his first successful personal computer company. Then, he founded NeXT, a computer platform development company. Then he bought a little computer graphics company, The Graphics Group, renamed it Pixar Animation Studios and proceeded to grow it into a pumpkin large enough to dominate Disney at the box office (until Disney caved and bought Pixar). Then he came back to Apple and introduced other groundbreaking technology—the iPod, iPhone and iPad—effectively launching a new curve every time.

Steve Jobs is a great modern example, but this process is not new. In fact, you can even find examples of this in ancient times (a little History Channel goes a long way). Now, entrepreneurship was not the norm in ancient Greece or Rome—those noble folks in the white robes and sandals thought it was beneath them. They weren't big on launching start-ups, know what I'm sayin'?

During a recent conversation with a friend (one of those PhD types), she drifted off into a history lesson, something she often does. She told me about this little-known entrepreneurial guy Pasion. (Yes, that was his real name.) He lived in Greece during the 4th century BC, and he was a slave. He worked his shackles off for these two bankers for basically no pay (sound familiar?) and eventually worked his way up to chief clerk at one of the branches in Athens. (I wonder where they parked the chariots?)

Pasion made the bank so profitable, the bankers set him free.

When they died, he bought the bank and very quickly became one of the richest men in Athens. He could have just handed the running of the bank over to slaves, or continued to slave away at it himself, but instead, he set up systems, and hired his right-hand man (also a freed slave) to run it for him.

Then, because he knew how to grow a behemoth pumpkin, the biggest pumpkin Athens had ever seen, he decided to do it again. (Okay, so they didn't *grow* pumpkins in Athens, but you've stayed with the metaphor this long, why get picky?) Pasion just had to plant another Atlantic Giant seed, so he launched a new business: a factory that made shields for the Athenian army. Way to start a new curve, Pasion! And smart, too. I mean, those Greeks and Romans sure did fight a lot.

Pasion grew a giant pumpkin for his masters, the bankers, and in turn grew it to an even bigger size after he bought it. Then, he started a new company—the shield factory—and applied his knowledge and influence to build it into another giant pumpkin. Success begets success. Even in ancient times.

However you choose to approach the next season of your business, it's key that you grow something from your handful of Atlantic Giant seeds. You're about to work really hard to implement your own Pumpkin Plan. You're about to get off the hamster wheel and free yourself from the all-too-common entrepreneurial trap. You're about to rock your clients' world and become the dominant force in your industry—a prize-winning behemoth of a pumpkin. That seed to your success is made of your innovation, hard work and genius—why would you want to start over?

Me? First, I built a computer repair business. Then, I built a computer crime investigation business. Then, I launched a behavioral website design business. Though different applications, all of my businesses are heavily technology-based. It's not just about building on your well of knowledge. It's about cultivating a habit of success.

You read this book. You know what to do. And when you put it into practice, you'll have the *experience* of working the Pumpkin Plan—you'll have the experience of success. And if you can be successful at one thing, you can be successful at other, similar things.

Passion begets persistence. You already have that. Persistence begets success. And success begets more success. When you've already grown a successful business, it's easier to build on that success to create a new product or service, or niche, or business that will be successful, too. They accept it. They *expect* it.

Nothing is constant except change. Working the Pumpkin Plan will not only save your business (and your life), it will help you grow a colossally successful business. But even those prizewinning giant pumpkins will finally die and rot. So, once you reach that pinnacle, you can't allow your business to become stagnant.

Next "season," whether that's next year, or ten years from now, let your Atlantic Giant seed work its magic as you grow yet another giant pumpkin.

CHAPTER FOURTEEN

HOW TO PUMPKIN PLAN *YOUR* BUSINESS — YOUR STORY

Throughout the book I've told eleven stories about how to Pumpkin Plan various industries. Now it's time to write your own story. How will you Pumpkin Plan your industry? How will you grow your own giant, *significant* pumpkin?

Employing the strategies that worked when you started your business won't get you a giant pumpkin. In the beginning, you had to trust your gut, say yes to all clients and opportunities, do the work yourself and fly by the seat of your pants. To grow the multimillion-dollar business you envisioned when you first opened your doors, you now need to kill what's not working, nurture what *is* working and develop systems to repeat the process. This is the essence of the Pumpkin Plan.

You have it in you to grow a remarkable business that attracts droves of clients worthy of your energy, time and great ideas. You have it in you to build a business that sets the standard in your industry. You have it in you to contribute to the world in a meaningful way—through innovation, by creating jobs, by setting an example of what is possible when you take a risk and go after your big, crazy, (and yes, attainable) dream. I believe in you. I do. I believe in you so much I wrote this book to *prove* to you that I believe in you.

The first step is simple and totally doable: fill out your Assessment Chart. If you move a few things around, you could even do it today. Before you know it, you'll have your own Pumpkin Plan story to tell. And I hope you'll send it to me when you do!

What are you waiting for?

Let's begin.

Thank you for reading *The Pumpkin Plan*. It is my deepest desire to help you achieve the business you envision. I hope *The Pumpkin Plan* has taken you one significant step closer to just that.

I would like to ask a small favor of you. No obligation, whatsoever:

Would you be willing to post an honest review of *The Pumpkin Plan*?

I ask because reviews are the most effective way for fellow entrepreneurs and business leaders to discover the book and determine if it will be of value to them. A review from you, even a single sentence or two, will achieve just that. To do it, simply go to the website (or the website for the store) where you bought the book and submit your review.

Again, I seek only your honest feedback. If you loved *The Pumpkin Plan*, please say so. If you loathed the book, please share that (just try to refrain from calling me bad names). And if you are indifferent about the book, share that, too.

What matters most is that fellow entrepreneurs hear your truth about *The Pumpkin Plan*.

Thank you. I am wishing you your most successful year yet!

—Mike

P.S. Not everyone who reads *The Pumpkin Plan* wants to go it alone. If you want the guidance of a certified Pumpkin Plan strategist, or even want to become one yourself, you can get more information at

PumpkinPlan.info.

ACKNOWLEDGMENTS

Every person I mention here is deserving of a greater thanks than just words can provide—an awkwardly long hug, a Cuban cigar and bottle of bubbly are probably more appropriate—but for now, acknowledging all of these amazing people will, hopefully, suffice.

First and foremost, I want to thank my writing partner, Anjanette Harper. I couldn't imagine a better team than you and me. I can't wait for your upcoming book (I heard it's a little bit racy and a lot a bit awesome). I will be the first in line to buy it.

A big hug and inappropriate public butt-cheek squeeze to my wife, Krista. Thanks for your unwavering support, especially when I tell you I have a great idea for a business book. . . about pumpkins. Tyler, Adayla and Jake. I love you guys. Hope this book doesn't embarrass you as much as the last one did. I can only imagine the ridicule you get when your dad writes about toilet paper and pumpkins and other bizarreness.

Thanks to my mom (unofficial sales ground force), my dad (unofficial legal counsel) and my big sis, Lisa (officially the biggest cheerleader I've got).

Zarik Boghossian—to know you is to love you. You are a great friend, a great mentor and a master at the barbecue. Keep that Nazook coming!!! A giant thanks to the folks who got the ball rolling on this book: my agent, Martha Kaplan, the yin to my yang, and to John Janstch, a kick-ass author and a generous friend.

Thank you to the folks at Penguin who've been nothing but welcoming and open to my crazy ideas, with a special shout out to my editor, Brooke Carey. This book is so much better for your insight . . . and probably a tad less obnoxious. Thanks to Denise Blasevick and the whole team at the S3 Agency, the marketing muscle behind this book. And thanks to Kevin Puls, an online, e-mail marketing maven.

This is where things get hairy, since there are thousands of other people I can think of who have helped make this a reality. So I simply ask you to forgive the broad strokes. . . . I want to thank the TPE (Toilet Paper Entrepreneur) community, the innovators and scrappers who continue to defy the odds and build kick-ass businesses. And to all the great folks who have been spreading the word for me and might not even know me personally, you are amazing and I can't thank you enough. Okay, I'll try: Thank you! Thank you from the bottom of my heart.

INDEX

Read more from Mike Michalowicz

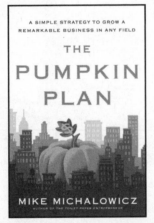